God's
END TIME
GENERATION
A New Generation

CHRIS FIRE

Copyright © 2011 by Revival Publishing

God's End-Time Generation:
A New Generation
by Chris Fire

All rights reserved.

Unless otherwise noted, all Scripture quotations are taken from the New King James Version. Copyright © 1982 by Thomas Nelson, Inc. Used by permission. All rights reserved.

Scripture quotations marked AMP are taken from the Amplified® Bible, Copyright © 1954, 1958, 1962, 1964, 1965, 1987 by The Lockman Foundation. Used by permission.

Scripture quotations marked KJV are taken from the King James Version of the Bible.

Scripture quotations marked NASB are taken from the New American Standard Bible®, Copyright © 1960, 1962, 1963, 1968, 1971, 1972, 1973, 1975, 1977, 1995 by The Lockman Foundation. Used by permission.

Scripture quotations marked NIV are taken from the HOLY BIBLE, NEW INTERNATIONAL VERSION. Copyright © 1973, 1978, 1984 by International Bible Society. Used by permission of Zondervan. All rights reserved.

FOREWORD

We are living in a period of great spiritual activity. As we approach the end of the age, both heaven and hell are intensifying their operations to accomplish their respective goals. Heaven seeks to rescue men and women from hell and to cause every knee and tongue to bow to Jesus Christ as Lord. Hell seeks to keep men in darkness and damnation. At such a critical time, the Church cannot afford to be at ease in Zion. The eternal destinies of multitudes hang in the balance. She must arise and play her role. Heaven needs her.

With this reality firmly in mind, Pastor Chris Fire, my spiritual son, has issued a call to the body of Christ to arise. Here are his words. "God is in the recruiting mode for a new generation that will be sanctified and dedicated to advancing the cause of Zion on the earth. Through prayer and the demonstration of His power, this remnant will claim the nations of the earth for Him." The task he sets out to accomplish in this book is to influence his readers to join God's end-time army to forcefully and vigilantly enforce God's agenda for this generation.

The core spiritual conviction of the author is obvious: We have a job to do—deliver human beings from eternal damnation. No other task is as urgent or as important. This job requires supernatural power. That power is available to those who will consecrate themselves and pray. Hence, the need of the hour is for people who are hungry enough to see God's kingdom come and souls saved that they will pay the price to appropriate the power needed to produce those results.

God's End-time Generation is a challenge to every believer to move from spiritual complacency and lukewarmness into a dynamic life lived under the influence and power of the Holy Spirit. Recognizing the times we live in, it calls for boldness in evangelism and a proactive aggressiveness that sadly is missing in too many Christians. This was the type of Spirit-generated boldness and aggressiveness that characterized the early church and made them so effective in turning their world "upside-down." Oh, how we need to see such boldness again in the church of Jesus Christ!

Pastor Fire is correct when he writes, "It is a great deception to live in a time of war yet act as though it is a time of peace. The church today is ignoring the sound of the trumpet and living casually in the time of war. I am not talking about a physical war, but the spiritual combat that we all face. We wrestle not against flesh and blood, but against principalities and powers in high places. The enemy has succeeded in penetrating and destroying many lives and ministries because the church has refused to pick up the mantle of a watchman on the wall."

My prayer is that all of God's people will heed the call being issued by this man of God that echoes God's own voice. And that the message of God's End-time Generation will be heard and repeated over and over again until the sleeping giant, the Church, awakens in the fullness of the power available to her in Christ.

You have in your hands a book that hell does not want read. But you cannot afford to ignore the signals sent from heaven concerning the days we live in. You and I must live in sync with the Spirit. And this book, dreaded in hell, but welcomed by heaven, will help us do so. So, if you are ready to be transformed, start reading. And if you are ready to be a part of a revolution, recommend it to someone else.

I believe heaven has declared a state of emergency for today, alerting its citizens, the body of Christ, to be vigilant and sober. Now more than ever, the citizens of the kingdom of God must be acutely aware of the spiritual realm."

Bishop Darlingston G. Johnson, D.Min, D.D.
Presiding Prelate, BWOMI

ACKNOWLEDGEMENTS

To my mother, Rose L'Amour, thank you for all your prayers and words of blessings. Let this book be a proof to you that God always answers prayer.

To my wife and kids, Thank you for allowing me to fulfill my calling. May heaven continue to shower you with blessings. I love you!

To the men and women of God that were placed on my path, thank you for the advice and support.

Finally, to all members of the Revival Center, thank you for your support and prayers, and for allowing me to share this gift with the body of Christ.

DEDICATION

I would like to dedicate this book to a special man of God in my life.

ArchBishop Duncan Williams, Action Chapel, for imparting in me the art of prayer and making me a battle axe in the hand of God. I know every time I stand to minister there is a deposit made into your heavenly account. You always have a special place in my heart. Thank you for never giving up on me. I always count it a privilege to have you have you in my life. I pray that I will always make you proud.

CONTENTS

Chapter 1:	The Remnant	13
Chapter 2:	The Devil Is Unleashed: Know His MO	19
Chapter 3:	State of Emergency	33
Chapter 4:	Know God for Yourself	39
Chapter 5:	No Compromise	45
Chapter 6:	Never Alone	53
Chapter 7:	A New Generation	57
Chapter 8:	You Are Unbreakable	63
Chapter 9:	The Spirit Upon	69
Chapter 10:	Fight or Faint	79
Chapter 11:	Finish Strong	89

CHAPTER 1
The Remnant

We are living in prophetic times and seasons as foretold by our Lord Jesus Christ, times of great signs, wonders, and the supernatural outpouring of the Holy Spirit. Even so, these are also times of great uncertainty and daunting challenges. Wars are erupting everywhere. Earthquakes, disasters, catastrophes, poverty, and diseases are destroying nations. Sin has exponentially increased, and the fear of God has diminished. Things once considered unacceptable are today declared normal.

Even worse, this paradigm shift has invaded the church and made it very difficult to make a clear distinction between believers and unbelievers. The church has relinquished her God-given authority to rule and have dominion on the earth. Instead of being the final authority on earth and providing direction to the world, the church is now looking to the world for direction.

There was a time when kings and rulers consulted the prophets of God to know how to govern the land. Today, however, rulers, governments, and even God's people are consulting mediums and psychics for direction and dabbling in witchcraft to gain power. Nevertheless, God in His infinite wisdom has always preserved a remnant that will fulfill His purposes on the earth and resist societal norms and pressures as they walk in complete obedience to Him.

In the early days of the Bible, God preserved Noah and his family though He destroyed the rest of the world with a great flood. Before the flood came, Noah warned an entire generation to repent of their wicked ways, yet not a single person heeded his warning. We know he warned an entire generation because the Bible states in Genesis 6:3, *"Then the LORD said, 'My Spirit will not contend with man forever, for he is mortal; his days will be a hundred and twenty years' "* (NIV). Shortly after, God gave Noah instructions on how to build the ark (a type of Christ) to preserve his life, his family, and all the animals—the remnant that would repopulate the earth and reestablish order.

King Nebuchadnezzar, ruler of the Neo-Babylonian Empire, destroyed Jerusalem and carried Israel into captivity. Nebuchadnezzar made a carved image and summoned the princes, governors, captains, judges, treasurers, counselors, sheriffs, and all the other rulers of the provinces to attend the dedication of the image. All were commanded to bow before the image at the sound of music. Everyone but three Hebrew boys obeyed the king's commands. Only Shadrach, Meshach, and Abednego refused to worship the image, choosing instead to honor God and risk being thrown into the furnace of fire.

The young Hebrews told the king their God was able to deliver them, but even if He did not, they still would not bow to the king's image. The king was furious and had them thrown into the furnace of fire. The heat was so intense that it killed the men who threw them into the furnace, but God was faithful and preserved His faithful ones.

Daniel 3:24–25, 27 tells us what happened next:

Then Nebuchadnezzar the king was astonished, and rose up in haste, and spake, and said unto his counselors, Did not we cast three men bound into the midst of the fire?

They answered and said unto the king, True, O king.
He answered and said, Lo, I see four men loose, walking in the midst of the fire, and they have no hurt; and the form of the fourth is like the Son of God. . . .

And the princes, governors, and captains, and the king's counselors, being gathered together, saw these men, upon whose bodies the fire had no power, nor was an hair of their head singed, neither were their coats changed, nor the smell of fire had passed on them. (KJV)

During King Ahab's reign over Israel, Queen Jezebel issued a decree to kill all God's prophets, but God preserved a remnant who refused to bow to Baal. In 1 Kings 19, the Bible gives account of Elijah, a prophet who demonstrated before the people of Israel and the prophets of Baal that the God of Israel was the true God. Subsequently, he ordered the execution of all the prophets of Baal.

Jezebel was wrought with anger when she heard of Elijah's activities and vowed to make an end to Elijah's life. Elijah, believing that Jezebel had killed all God's prophets and he was next in line, ran for his life. Then God spoke to Elijah, *"Yet I reserve seven thousand in Israel—all whose knees have not bowed down to Baal and all whose mouths have not kissed him"* (1 Kings 19:18, NIV).

In the days of our Lord Jesus Christ, the remnant was the disciples who followed Christ's teachings faithfully and set themselves apart to fulfill His purpose. In the book of Revelation, we see another remnant; too many to number, they are referred to as a "great crowd." The truth is, in every generation from Bible times until today, God has always preserved a remnant. The question is, are you or do you want to be a part of the remnant?

During my prayer time, God spoke to me to sound the trumpet and wake up His people; that is why I have written this book. God is in the recruiting mode for a new generation that will be sanctified and dedicated to advancing the cause of Zion on the earth. Through prayer and the demonstration of His power, this remnant will claim the nations of the earth for Him.

There is a longing in the world for truth and direction. Unfortunately, this longing has triggered the growth of many false religious sects. People are in search of the truth, but they are looking in the wrong places. The Bible declares that all creation, meaning all people and all living creatures, is waiting earnestly for the manifestation of the sons of God (Rom. 8:19). But only God's sons (this term includes both males and females) have what the world is looking for—Jesus.

God's end-time remnant is a generation like no other, a new breed made up of the true sons of God. These are sons who are zealous about pleasing their Father. They look like their Father, and they hate what He hates and love what He loves. They will not bow to the dictates of this world's system, which promotes indulgence in sin and wickedness.

This end-time generation that God is raising supersedes culture, race, country, color, and denomination. This end-time generation does not belong to a particular church or denomination. It's not about who your pastor is or where you go to church; it's about who your God is and whom you serve.

God's end-time generation is His possession. They belong to Him, and they live for Him. They are people who love Him and are determined to glorify Him in every area of their lives, no matter what it takes. God has His eyes on this generation because it is His last weapon to pull down strongholds, to set captives free, to proclaim His love and mercy to the nations of the world, and to fulfill the mandate of preaching the gospel until Jesus Christ appears in the clouds of glory. Simply put, God's end-time generation is radical.

Are you a son? Are you a true son? If so, heaven depends on you, and the whole earth is waiting on you. Are you ready for the challenge? Then let's wage war!

CHAPTER 2
The Devil is Unleashed: Know His MO

Revelation 12:7–12 reads:

And war broke out in heaven: Michael and his angels fought with the dragon; and the dragon and his angels fought, but they did not prevail, nor was a place found for them in heaven any longer. So the great dragon was cast out, that serpent of old, called the Devil and Satan, who deceives the whole world; he was cast to the earth, and his angels were cast out with him.

Then I heard a loud voice saying in heaven, "Now salvation, and strength, and the kingdom of our God, and the power of His Christ have come, for the accuser of our brethren, who accused them before our God day and night, has been cast down. And they overcame him by the blood of the Lamb and by the word of their testimony, and they did not love their lives to the death. Therefore rejoice, O heavens, and you who dwell in them! Woe to the inhabitants of the earth and the sea! For the devil has come down to you, having great wrath, because he knows that he has a short time."

In Revelation 12, the Bible talks about a war that took place in heaven between the archangel Michael (the minister of defense) and the dragon (the devil). This war occurred in the pre-Adamic world and resulted in the devil's banishment from heaven because of his rebellion. Revelation 12:12 stresses the urgency of this enemy's mission: "For the devil has come down to you, having great wrath, because he knows that he has a short time." However, the church today underestimates the length, the depth, and the width of this enemy we are fighting.

In Isaiah 14, the Bible refers to the devil as an "angel of light." He was originally an archangel assigned to praise and worship in heaven. Through his rebellion, he deceived one-third of the angels serving the almighty God and convinced them to join him in rebellion against God. If the devil was able to seduce that many angels in heaven, where the very presence of God dwells, then that gives you a glimpse of the kind of enemy we are dealing with. I am not lifting the enemy above our God, and neither am I trying to praise his strength; but the Bible says we must know our enemy and his devices lest he gain advantage over us.

He knows his time is short so he has intensified his onslaught against the church. The serpent that Adam and Eve dealt with in Genesis has transformed into a dragon in the apocalyptic era in which we find ourselves. While the nature of the warfare has shifted with time, the enemy's goal, to steal God's glory, remains unchanged. If we are to wage effective warfare we have to understand the tactics that the enemy employs to achieve his desired end result, the glory of God. In the natural, armies win battles by knowing the strategies of their enemies and creating counter strategies to subvert their enemies' plans. Similarly, the end-time generation must know the enemy's MO, his mode of operation, in order to be relevant and effective. In John 10:10, Jesus exposed the threefold strategy of the enemy: *"The thief [devil] comes only to steal, kill, and destroy."*

TO STEAL

Perhaps the most dangerous part of the enemy's mission is his intent to steal. It is the most dangerous because it is the most subtle; it can easily go undetected. If the enemy is able to conquer at this level, then he is able to subdue and achieve his ultimate goal, which is receiving the glory due to God alone.

The devil has coveted this glory from the very beginning when he was still in heaven. God, however, is jealous of His glory. In Isaiah 42:8, God says He will not give His glory to another. The only way to make God's glory greater is to increase the number of people who will give it to Him.

The book of Revelation speaks about the magnificent glory shown to God in His heavenly home:

Now when He had taken the scroll, the four living creatures and the twenty-four elders fell down before the Lamb, each having a harp, and golden bowls full of incense, which are the prayers of the saints. And they sang a new song, saying:

"You are worthy to take the scroll,
And to open its seals; For You were slain,
And have redeemed us to God by Your blood,
Out of every tribe and tongue and people and nation, And have made us kings and priests to our God;
And we shall reign on the earth."

Then I looked, and I heard the voice of many angels around the throne, the living creatures, and the elders; and the number of them was ten thousand times ten thousand, and thousands of thousands, saying with a loud voice:

"Worthy is the Lamb who was slain
To receive power and riches and wisdom,
And strength and honor and glory and blessing!"
—Revelation 5:8–12

After these things I looked, and behold, a great multitude which no one could number, of all nations, tribes, peoples, and tongues, standing before the throne and before the Lamb, clothed with white robes, with palm branches in their hands, and crying out with a loud voice, saying, "Salvation belongs to our God who sits on the throne, and to the Lamb!" All the angels stood around the throne and the elders and the four living creatures, and fell on their faces before the throne and worshiped God, saying:

"Amen! Blessing and glory and wisdom,
Thanksgiving and honor and power and might,
Be to our God forever and ever.
Amen."

—Revelation 7:9–12

According to these Scripture passages, there are four categories in heaven that give God the glory: the twenty-four elders, four creatures, the angels, and the great crowd. The numbers for the twenty-four elders and the four creatures are forever fixed. Those numbers will never change. Neither can we change the number of angels. So the only group that we can influence is the great crowd. We can impact that category by increasing the number of people giving God glory in the earthly realm, and the only way to increase that number is through salvation.

Psalm 21:5 says, *"His glory is great in thy salvation: honor and majesty hast thou laid upon him"* (KJV). Furthermore the bible lets us know in the book of Habakkuk 2:14 that, *"The earth shall be filled with the knowledge of the glory of the Lord, as the waters cover the sea..."* It is the desire of God that the whole earth be covered with his Glory;

Hence, the first mission of the enemy is to steal the salvation of multitudes. Jesus, by shedding His blood, has already appropriated salvation for all. There is nothing the enemy can do to prevent the gift of salvation. It was finished when Christ took his final agonizing breath and said, "It is finished." The only thing the enemy can do now is to try to hinder multitudes from realizing that the gift of salvation is available or to try to prevent them from receiving it. He does this by controlling access to the gateways of nations and by exploiting the complacency of born-again Christians.

There are still many people in diverse nations who have never heard the gospel of Jesus Christ. In some cases, their governments have prevented the message of the gospel of Jesus Christ from being shared via missionaries, evangelists, and mass media. In other cases, there are not enough missionaries willing to leave their comfort zones to win the souls that are waiting. Additionally, many believers do not consider winning souls their responsibility. They have become complacent in their spiritual walk and negligent in their God-given mandate to win souls, though people everywhere are hungry for the gospel of Jesus Christ.

When I talk to believers, I like to ask them how often they share Christ with someone. You might be surprised to know that few people share Christ on a consistent basis. People have all kinds of reasons why they don't believe it is their responsibility to win souls for the kingdom of God, but none of these excuses are valid. A day shouldn't pass without your witnessing to someone. As a great man of God once said, evangelism is our supreme task. Whenever you miss on witnessing, you forfeit your purpose on earth.

The other tactic the enemy uses to prevent people from receiving salvation is his age-old use of deception. Second Corinthians 4:3–4 states it for us: *"And even if our gospel is veiled, it is veiled to those who are perishing, in whose case the god of this world has blinded the minds of the unbelieving, that they might not see the light of the gospel of the glory of Christ who is the image of God."*

The enemy works to make it impossible for unbelievers to see the light of the gospel. He bombards them with gross darkness in an attempt to block the entrance of light into their souls. The result is a generation or a nation devoid of light and endorsing all kinds of sinful acts such as idol worship, abortion, homosexuality, adultery, fornication, and the list goes on and on. The enemy deceives unbelievers by making them think (1) they can live by their own standards and do what is right in their own eyes without eternal repercussions; and (2) if something feels good, then it is okay to do it. But we know the wages of sin is death; only God's gift of salvation provides eternal life.

The Bible says a man who has sons will not be ashamed when he stands to contend at the enemy's gate (Psalm 127:5). The true sons of God will arise and contend with the enemy for the souls of the nations. The true sons of God will possess the enemy's gates so that the gospel may access the hearts of the captives behind the gates. Are you a true son?

Isaiah 66:18–20 declares: *"For I know their works and their thoughts; the time is coming to gather all nations and tongues and they shall come to see my glory. And I will set a sign among them and will send survivors from them to nations . . . to distant coastlands that have neither heard My fame nor seen my glory. And they will declare my glory among the nations."* Are you a survivor? Do you have eternal life? If so, the mandate is yours to declare the glory of God among the nations.

Those of the end-time generation bear two main responsibilities. First, they are to ensure the entrance of the Word of God into the nations: *"The entrance of the word gives light and understanding to the simple"* (Psalm 119:30).

The bible lets us know that the ministry that God gave us, the ministry we are accountable for, is the ministry of reconciliation.

Now all things are of God, who has reconciled us to Himself through Jesus Christ, and has given us the ministry of reconciliation, that is, that God was in Christ reconciling the world to Himself, not imputing their trespasses to them, and has committed to us the word of reconciliation.

Now then, we are ambassadors for Christ, as though God were pleading through us: we implore you on Christ's behalf, be reconciled to God.
–2 Corinthians 5:18-20.

God has given us a ministry of reconciliation, no matter what office you sit in, or don't sit in, at the end of the day our ultimate goal has to be to reconcile others to God by giving them the word of reconciliation. We have a responsibility as ambassadors for Christ to take the word of reconciliation to the nations. Until we understand this ministry, the ministry of reconciliation, the importance of giving the word of reconciliation, we will be very busy in the body of Christ doing other ministries (plural), and neglect the true ministry (singular), that God has committed unto us.

We have to take the word of reconciliation to the nations. They are ready. The harvest is ripe and ready to be reaped. We are his hands and feet. We are his heart. We have to assume this awesome responsibility of taking the gospel, the word of reconciliation into the nations. Only then will light emerge and darkness be conquered.

Secondly those who are of the end-time generation bear the responsibility of possessing the nations. God said, *"Ask of me and*

I will give you the nations as your inheritance and the uttermost parts of the earth as your possession" (Psalm. 2:8). We have to come to a place where we possess our possessions. The bible says that once we go from salvation, to deliverance, righteousness and holiness, the next step is to possess our possessions.

"But on Mount Zion there shall be deliverance,
And there shall be holiness;
The house of Jacob shall possess their possessions."
–Obadiah 1:17

In the book of Revelations 17, John the revelator is shown a profound vision that I believe portray a vivid relationship between the body of Christ possession its possession and the souls in the nation. He was shown the image of a woman sitting on a beast with seven heads and ten horns. The angel of the Lord then explain the vision as follows:

"Here is the mind which has wisdom: The seven heads are seven mountains on which the woman sits. There are also seven kings. Five have fallen, one is, and the other has not yet come. And when he comes, he must continue a short time. The beast that was, and is not, is himself also the eighth, and is of the seven, and is going to perdition.

"The ten horns which you saw are ten kings who have received no kingdom as yet, but they receive authority for one hour as kings with the beast. These are of one mind, and they will give their power and authority to the beast. These will make war with the Lamb, and the Lamb will overcome them, for He is Lord of lords and King of kings; and those who are with Him are called, chosen, and faithful."

Then he said to me, "The waters which you saw, where the harlot sits, are peoples, multitudes, nations, and tongues.
–Revelations 17:9-15

Notice the whore was not above the water, nor was she in the water. The bible says she sits upon the waters, which are the souls. This lets me know that a part of her body was in the air, and another part was touching the waters. In other words she dominated the airways, and she dominated the waters. The air and the water are the gateways to the nations. You either go by plane or by ship. As long as this whore is sitting on the waters, we will never realize the abundant harvest. In order to get to the souls, the whore must be overthrown, and for that whore to be over thrown we must engage into a spiritual warfare..

When God's end-time generation sees the nations, and everything in it as their possession, and take it back from the kingdom of darkness by force; When they are willing to leave their comfort zone and bring the word of reconciliation to the nations, the enemy's tactic to steal salvation is thwarted.

TO KILL

If the enemy is not able to steal, then he takes the offensive and tries to kill. What is the enemy afraid of and thus wants to kill? He is afraid of the prophetic word over our lives. One of the main assignments of the spirit of death, therefore, is to silence the prophetic voice.

To illustrate, let's look at the way the enemy tried to kill the prophetic word in the life of Moses and in the life of Jesus Christ.

MOSES

Exodus 1:6–9 reads: *"Now Joseph and all his brothers and all that generation died, but the Israelites were fruitful and multiplied greatly and became exceedingly numerous so that the land was filled with them. Then a new king, who did not know about Joseph, came to power in Egypt. 'Look,' he said to his people, 'the Israelites have become much too numerous for us' "* (NIV).

Verses 15 and 16 continue: *"The king of Egypt said to the Hebrew midwives, whose names were Shiphrah and Puah, 'When you help the Hebrew women in childbirth and observe them on the delivery stool, if it is a boy kill him; but if it is a girl, let her live' "* (NIV).

According to verse 17, *"the midwives, however, feared God and did not do what the king had told them to do"* (NIV). In response, *"the king of Egypt summoned the midwives and asked them, 'Why have you let the boys live?' "* (v. 18, NIV). The story concludes in verse 22: *"Then Pharaoh gave this order to all his people, 'Every boy that is born must be thrown into the Nile, but let the girls live' "* (NIV).

After Pharaoh issued this decree, Moses, the son of a Levite man and woman, and a descendant of Abraham, was born. Moses had already been chosen by God to lead His people out of Egypt and into the land of Canaan. But even before his birth, the enemy knew that the child of promise who would fulfill the prophetic word given to Abraham would be born, so he tried to kill the prophetic word before it could take root. His tactic was twofold: (1) He tried to kill all the males, the carriers of the seed, to prevent the descendants of Abraham from multiplying. (2) He tried to kill Moses, the specific person destined to lead the descendants of Abraham out of Egypt and into the Promised Land.

JESUS

Jesus' situation was similar to that of Moses. After Adam and Eve were deceived and disobeyed God, God cursed the serpent and then prophesied, saying, *"I will put enmity between you and the woman, between your offspring and hers; he will crush your head and you will strike his heel"* (Gen. 3:15). Jesus was the offspring who would crush the serpent's head; consequently, in Matthew 2:16, Herod gave orders to kill all the boys of Bethlehem and its vicinity who were two years old and under, which would have included Jesus.

The devil is after the prophetic word over your life and the life of nations. If killing the prophetic word means taking your life, he will try to do it. If it means creating events and circumstances to prevent you from walking in the prophetic word, he will do it. For instance, you may be called to preach the gospel to the nations as a missionary, but the enemy may try to hinder that call by creating debt in your life. He may try to control your advancement in the kingdom of God by obligating you to creditors and putting you in a position where you have to constantly work to repay your debts. The same circumstance could be true of someone who is called to finance the gospel. Maybe the reason God said "My peace I give to you" was to nullify the enemy's attempts to create situations (like debt) that cause us to lose our peace.

One of God's prophetic words regarding nations is that the earth shall be filled with the knowledge of the glory of God as the waters cover the sea. The enemy fights this word by making it difficult to spread the gospel in certain nations. But as God's end-time generation, we must engage the prophetic word over the nations and pray them into manifestation. We already have heaven's backing.

We must invoke the powers of heaven on our behalves for the manifestation of the prophetic word, both for ourselves and for the nations, through intense, relentless, intercessory prayer. This is the type of prayer that brought Moses and Jesus Christ onto the scene.

Exodus 2:23 records, *"Now it came about in the course of those many days that the king of Egypt died. And the sons of Israel sighed because of the bondage, and they cried out; and their cry for help because of their bondage rose up to God."* A few verses later, in the next chapter, we see God's answer to that prayer:

And the LORD said: "I have surely seen the oppression of My people who are in Egypt, and have heard their cry because of their taskmasters, for I know their sorrows. So I have come down to deliver them out of the hand of the Egyptians, and to bring them up from that land to a good and large land, to a land flowing with milk and honey, to the place of the Canaanites and the Hittites and the Amorites and the Perizzites and the Hivites and the Jebusites. Now therefore, behold, the cry of the children of Israel has come to Me, and I have also seen the oppression with which the Egyptians oppress them. Come now, therefore, and I will send you to Pharaoh that you may bring My people, the children of Israel, out of Egypt."
— Exodus 3:7–10

Many people of different dispensations on various occasions have cried out for the Savior of Israel, Jesus Christ. One was a prophetess named Anna: *"Now there was one, Anna, a prophetess, the daughter of Phanuel, of the tribe of Asher. She was of a great age, and had lived with a husband seven years from her virginity; and this woman was a widow of about eighty-four years, who did not depart from the temple, but served God with fastings and prayers night and day. And coming in that instant she gave thanks to the Lord, and spoke of Him to all those who looked for redemption in Jerusalem"* (Luke 2:36–38). Until we, like Anna, arise in the place of intensive, desperate, and agonizing prayer, the devil will always kill the prophetic word in our lives. Full of the promises of God, we will yet see no manifestation of them, because the only way to see the manifestation of the prophetic word is through prayer.

TO DESTROY

The ultimate goal of the enemy is to destroy our lives; in fact, he is sometimes called the "destroyer." The word destroy simply means to eradicate, annihilate, and to bring to the point of no repair.

I originally thought the Bible should say that the enemy comes to steal, destroy, and kill—in that order—but the Holy Spirit showed me that destroying has a greater impact than killing. If something is stolen, it can be recovered; if something dies, it can be resurrected and restored to its original state (look at Lazarus). But if something is destroyed, it is beyond the point of repair; it must be completely reconstructed or rebuilt.

When the Philistines prevailed over Samson, his life and ministry were destroyed. If you read his story closely, you'll see he had to start all over again. His hair needed to grow long again, and his strength needed to increase again before he could avenge his enemies. Similarly, the enemy's goal is to destroy us, because anytime he succeeds in destroying any area of our lives, he brings us back to the starting line. This forces us to invest additional time into rebuilding something we once had. This is the sad reality for so many people who are rebuilding their lives, their relationships, their businesses, or other things they once had.

But I am grateful that the God we serve has made provision in His Word for any weapon that the enemy throws at us. It is not the end of everything when things in our lives are destroyed. We can still pick up the broken pieces and start over again, because our God is the God of second chances. When Samson's life was destroyed and he was a slave of his enemies, he cried out to God for a second chance. God restored his hair, which represented his strength. The Bible goes on to say that in the end Samson killed more Philistines than he had ever killed during all the previous years.

The enemy comes to steal, kill, and destroy, but Christ came that we may have eternal life and have it to its fullness. Once we truly understand Christ's gift of eternal life, we will be able to fight for the manifestation of that life in every dimension of our lives. If a situation seems impossible, it becomes possible once we receive the gift of life. If peace is absent, the full life of Christ ushers it in. If poverty abounds , the life of Christ brings riches. In Christ, the fullness of life overcomes every attempt of the enemy to steal, kill, and destroy.

CHAPTER 3
State of Emergency

When a fire alarm sounds in a building, you have to vacate the premises, no matter what you are doing. In a national state of emergency, a government issues a declaration to alert its citizens of impending danger and to recommend ways for them to alter their normal behaviors and actions. For instance, after the September 11 terrorist attack, the U.S. government began alerting its citizens to possible terrorism through the use of various codes. Code orange represented a high terrorist risk, and whenever a code orange was issued, everyone was urged to pay extra attention to his or her surroundings.

I believe heaven has declared a state of emergency for today, alerting its citizens, the body of Christ, to be vigilant and sober. Now more than ever, the citizens of the kingdom of God must be acutely aware of the spiritual realm. Many, however, are ignoring the signals sent from heaven and living their lives out of sync with God's divine timing.

UNDERSTANDING THE TIMES

First Chronicles 12:32 says, "Of the sons of Issachar who had understanding of the times, to know what Israel ought to do, their chiefs were two hundred; and all their brethren were at their command" (emphasis added). Understanding the times is a critical skill for every human being, both in the natural and the spiritual realms. Knowing the times physically, for example, enables us to dress properly and plan accordingly. We do not wear summer clothes in winter or winter clothes in summer if we want to be comfortable and able to function in the season at hand.

Just as there is physical time, there is also spiritual time, Although most people understand physical timetables, they often lack understanding of the spiritual calendar. But the sons of Issachar understood the times and seasons in the spiritual realm; and as a result, they always knew what Israel needed to do and had their brothers at their command. By understanding the times, they were able to access the thoughts and mind of God and provide direction to the people of Israel.

The understanding of spiritual times is granted to those who spend time with God in prayer. When you read though the Scriptures, you will note that every person who had an understanding of time was a person of prayer and intercession. Daniel was one such person. Because he understood the times, Daniel was led to intercede for Israel's release from captivity: *"In the first year of his reign I, Daniel, understood by the books the number of the years specified by the word of the LORD through Jeremiah the prophet, that He would accomplish seventy years in the desolations of Jerusalem. Then I set my face toward the Lord God to make request by prayer and supplications, with fasting, sackcloth, and ashes"* (Dan. 9:2–3).

Daniel was referring to the scripture in Jeremiah 25:11 that states, *"And this whole land will be a desolation and a horror, and these nations will serve the king of Babylon seventy years"* (NASB). Daniel understood it was the appointed time for God to move among the children of Israel, since they had already been in captivity for seventy years. He thus engaged himself in prayer and fasting to see God move and set His people free.

I believe the reason so many Christians go through life confused and disoriented is that they don't spend time in prayer and therefore do not understand the times and seasons of their lives. But when you understand the spiritual time, you are better equipped to positively handle situations and circumstances in natural time, since the spiritual always supersedes and controls the natural.

Even demons possess this understanding of the times. We see this illustrated in Matthew 8:28–29: *"When he arrived at the other side in the region of the Gadarenes, two demon-possessed men coming from the tombs met him. They were so violent that no one could pass that way. 'What do you want with us, Son of God?' they shouted. 'Have you come here to torture us before the appointed time?'"*

This subject of understanding the times is so critical because when you lack divine understanding, you'll miss your time of visitation. In Matthew 16:2–4, Jesus stated this clearly to the Pharisees: *"When it is evening you say, 'It will be fair weather, for the sky is red'; and in the morning, 'It will be foul weather today, for the sky is red and threatening.' Hypocrites! You know how to discern the face of the sky, but you cannot discern the signs of the times. A wicked and adulterous generation seeks after a sign, and no sign shall be given to it except the sign of the prophet Jonah."*

Jesus called the Pharisees "hypocrites" because they knew how to discern physical times but lacked understanding of spiritual times. They knew the Messiah was coming, and they were waiting for Him; but because they never understood God's timing, they missed the time of their visitation.

REDEEMING THE TIME

Ephesians 5:15–21 provides quite a bit of instruction about the wise use of time. Let's read the passage in its entirety and then examine it verse by verse:

"See then that you walk circumspectly, not as fools but as wise, redeeming the time, because the days are evil."

"Therefore do not be unwise, but understand what the will of the Lord is. And do not be drunk with wine, in which is dissipation; but be filled with the Spirit, speaking to one another in psalms and hymns and spiritual songs, singing and making melody in your heart to the Lord, giving thanks always for all things to God the Father in the name of our Lord Jesus Christ, submitting to one another in the fear of God."

The apostle Paul in Ephesians 5 talks about the need for the children of God to separate themselves from any kind of sin. In verse 15, he says, *"See then that you walk circumspectly, not as fools but as wise."* This lets us know that in this life we can walk either as fools or as wise children of God. Paul encourages us to walk as the wise, but

HOW DOES A WISE PERSON WALK?

The answer is in verse 16: *"redeeming the time, because the days are evil."* Another translation urges us to take advantage of every opportunity. Now is not the time for us to sit down and allow every opportunity to share the gospel to pass us by. We don't know if we are the last ones the Lord sends to share the good news with a particular individual. We can no longer sit in our churches and hope the same couple of visitors will come back on Sunday morning and hopefully give their lives to Christ one day. It's time to take Jesus into our communities, workplaces, streets, and public places. It's time to be aggressive with the gospel. The devil is not wasting time, and neither should we.

You may agree that we should redeem the time but wonder how to do it since time is a perishable gift. In verse 17 of our passage, the apostle gives the key to redeeming the time: understanding God's will. We live in times where we cannot afford to miss the will of God for our lives, families, cities, communities, and nations. If we want to redeem the time, we need to first understand the plan of God for our lives and then begin to walk in that plan.

I have come to realize that the first and most important plan God has for all His children is for them to share the gospel and win souls. It is the main reason why you and I are still here on earth. I once told a preacher that both God and the devil are souls oriented. Everything God does in and through us is to create an opportunity to reach more souls for the kingdom, and everything the devil does is aimed at keeping one more soul in darkness. For instance, if God's plan is to reach your coworker through you, but every day you pass the person by and never talk about Jesus, you are denying that individual the opportunity to be saved. Unless you understand the will of God for you, you will not be proactive and make every second of your existence on earth count.

WHERE ARE THE MIGHTY MEN?

The mighty men in Christ today are distracted, slumbering watchmen who need to wake up. An alert rings out from heaven itself to rouse the mighty men: *"Proclaim this among the nations: prepare a war; rouse the mighty men! Let all the soldiers draw near, let them come up! Beat your plowshares into swords and your pruning hooks into spears; let the weak say, 'I am a mighty man'"* (Joel 3:9–10).

It is a great deception to live in a time of war yet act as though it is a time of peace. The church today is ignoring the sound of the trumpet and living casually in the time of war. I am not talking about a physical war, but the spiritual combat that we all face. We wrestle not against flesh and blood, but against principalities and powers in high places. The enemy has succeeded in penetrating and destroying many lives and ministries because the church has refused to pick up the mantle of a watchman on the wall.

The Bible says in the last days evil will increase. Indeed, our adversary, the devil, has launched an all-out attack against the people of God. There are increased natural disasters, diseases, sicknesses, divorces, drugs, and suicides, and a significant decrease in the manifestations of the promises of God in people's lives.

God is saying to us today: "The enemy has been rising against My people, their families, and loved ones. The enemy is after your case, and I need a man or a woman who can wage war against the devil through prayer and warfare. I need a voice in Zion that can cry out and contend for the destinies of churches, families, communities, cities and nations."

Thus wherever you are, child of God, I say to you, "Wake up, in the name of Jesus! Come out of your sleep, pick up your sword, and drive the devil out of your family, church, community, and nation" In Jesus' name, may it be so!

CHAPTER 4
Know God for Yourself

The Bible speaks of King Nebuchadnezzar, who built a carved image and compelled all citizens in Babylon to worship it at the sound of the trumpet. This was a satanic decree to prohibit the people who knew the true Jehovah from worshiping Him:

Nebuchadnezzar responded and said to them, "Is it true, Shadrach, Meshach and Abed-nego, that you do not serve my gods or worship the golden image that I have set up?

Now if you are ready, at the moment you hear the sound of the horn, flute, lyre, trigon, psaltery and bagpipe and all kinds of music, to fall down and worship the image that I have made, very well. But if you do not worship, you will immediately be cast into the midst of a furnace of blazing fire; and what god is there who can deliver you out of my hands?"

Shadrach, Meshach and Abed-nego replied to the king, "O Nebuchadnezzar, we do not need to give you an answer concerning this matter. If it be so, our God whom we serve is able to deliver us from the furnace of blazing fire; and He will deliver us out of your hand, O king. But even if He does not, let it be known to you, O king, that we are not going to serve your gods or worship the golden image that you have set up."
—Daniel 3:14–18, NASB

There are satanic laws and decrees being passed in nations today to force people into idolatry or compliance by preventing them from worshiping the true God. Let me submit to you, beloved, that the enemy will always challenge your relationship with God. By relationship, I am not talking about quoting Scripture or knowing about God, but having a close and deep connection with Him.

We are living in times of great confusion, and it is unfortunate that even Christians sometimes lose sight of who God is and what He can do for them. The three Hebrew boys responded to the king by saying "our God." This lets us know they had a personal relationship with God; they knew the God they were serving and seeking. Our knowledge of God must be birthed out of our relationship with Him. We cannot say we know God unless we have experienced Him.

The fact that people come to church or quote Scripture does not necessarily mean they know God. I was praying one night and asking God why we no longer see the miracles of old. Why do we see fewer healings, deliverances, and signs and wonders in the church? The Holy Spirit clearly answered that it is due to our lack of relationship with God.

When you are in close relationship with someone—an intimate relationship—it requires a large expenditure of time. Spending an hour a day in prayer is the most basic step for every believer. But the Spirit of God opened my eyes to the revelation of tithing everything, including time. I know we usually limit tithing to finances, but I believe we need to give God a tithe of our time as well. Since there are twenty-four hours in a day, we should spend at least two hours and forty minutes a day in prayer (or just round it up to three hours of prayer). I believe this is why people in the Bible who walked closely with God were able to fast for forty days, which represents a tithe of a year. In fact, in my opinion, a minister of the gospel must be able to fast a minimum of forty days throughout a year.

FRUITS OF INTIMACY

Hearing God

In my few years in ministry, I have encountered many Christians who struggle to hear God. In my opinion, this results from relegating the job of hearing from God to pastors, prophets, and leaders while failing to realize that God desires an intimate relationship with each and every one of us. The Bible says that in times of old, God spoke through prophets, but now He has spoken through His Son, Jesus Christ (Heb. 1:1–2).

Every believer must develop the ability to hear the voice of God. The ability to hear God's voice is proof of knowing Him. I know my wife so well that I can recognize her voice without even seeing her. I know how she sounds and expresses herself. The same holds true in our relationship with God.

John 10:4 says, *"And when he brings out his own sheep, he goes before them; and the sheep follow him, for they know his voice."* The reason sheep recognize their shepherd's voice and follow him is simply that they have developed a relationship with him. Until we develop a relationship with God through salvation and continual prayer, we will never be able to hear the voice of the Master.

In these end times, many strange voices will arise to seduce the elite. It becomes even more critical, therefore, for Christians to learn to hear God for themselves. But we have unfortunately created a church where believers think only the pastors and prophets can hear God and therefore wait for them to step into the pulpit on Sundays to let the believers know what God has said. This scenario was indeed true in the Old Testament, where God spoke to His people through the prophets and priests; but in the New Testament, the veil was removed to grant to any person who believes the privilege to enter into God's presence and know Him intimately. I am not undermining the role of pastors and prophets, but God's intention in the New Testament was for His people to have a personal relationship with Him.

God desires to communicate with us directly. Hebrews 1:1–3 explains this beautifully: "God, who at various times and in various ways spoke in time past to the fathers by the prophets, has in these last days spoken to us by His Son, whom He has appointed heir of all things, through whom also He made the worlds; who being the brightness of His glory and the express image of His person, and upholding all things by the word of His power, when He had by Himself purged our sins, sat down at the right hand of the Majesty on high." Furthermore, the bible lets us know that there is one mediator between God and man, and that is Jesus. We have to know him for ourselves and that only happens when we are intimate with him.

Boldness

Boldness is a natural outflow of an intimate relationship with God that gives us the assurance that we act with the backing of heaven. Boldness is a critical attribute to possess because sometimes God will call us to do things that do not make sense to the rational mind.

In this new generation, God expects us to boldly challenge certain traditions and rituals in order to bring change and restoration. It took boldness for Gideon to destroy the altar in his father's house that had been established for years. It took boldness for Deborah to serve as judge for the people of Israel and to restore the land. It took boldness for David to challenge and defeat Goliath. And it will take boldness for you to fulfill your destiny and purpose.

I like Acts 4:13 and 29. These two verses make clear the connection between boldness and relationship with Jesus. Verse

13 says, "Now when they saw the boldness of Peter and John, and perceived that they were uneducated and untrained men, they marveled. And they realized that they had been with Jesus." Verse 29 shows the disciples' response in prayer: "Now, Lord, look on their threats, and grant to Your servants that with all boldness they may speak Your word." Without boldness, the early church leaders could never have accomplished their God-given purpose, and that boldness came only because of the relationship they had with Jesus. It is the same for us.

Godliness

Godliness is one of the attributes that characterizes those who know God. Godliness is an inner piety; it's an inner desire to live for God and please Him. Today, however, many professed believers do not live godly lives, and because they have little desire to please Him, they thus exhibit little reverential fear of Him.

Paul warned Timothy about those who have a form of godliness but renounce its power: "But reject profane and old wives' fables, and exercise yourself toward godliness. For bodily exercise profits a little, but godliness is profitable for all things, having promise of the life that now is and of that which is to come. This is a faithful saying and worthy of all acceptance" (1 Timothy. 4:7–9).

It is impossible for us to have an intimate relationship with God and not be godly. The bible lets us know that when Jesus was betrayed and Peter denied association with Jesus, a woman said, concerning Peter, "he was with him (Jesus) because he sounds like him (Jesus)."

It is important for us to not just put on a face of godliness but to actually desire to please God in everything we do. When considering a specific action, the question we need to ask is, does this action please God? Remember, the only way to stand for godliness is to exercise yourself in godliness.

Doing Exploits

Daniel 11:32 says, *"Those who do wickedly against the covenant he shall corrupt with flattery; but the people who know their God shall be strong, and carry out great exploits."* Our ability to carry out exploits stems from our knowledge of God. The knowledge of God comes by prayer and meditation of the Word. That's why the enemy exerts his best effort to rob Christians of their times of prayer and meditation.

More and more churches all across America are setting aside less and less time for prayer and intercession. However, the less we know God, the more we see our challenges as impossible. But the more we serve Him, His house, and His people, the more our knowledge of Him increases and the more our relationship with Him flourishes.

CHAPTER 5
No Compromise

The three Hebrew boys in Daniel 3 were models of uncompromising loyalty and commitment to God. Boldly they declared to Nebuchadnezzar, *"Let it be known to you, O king, that we do not serve your gods, nor will we worship the gold image which you have set up"* (v. 3).

Compromise is an attitude of the heart found in people who want to fit in and not stand out in order to avoid criticism, mockery, and all kinds of pressure. This syndrome will always lead compromise.

I define compromise simply as anything you do not in line with who you really are (identity). I believe the spirit of compromise is one of the enemy's primary weapons in our day. Every believer should be able to discern this spirit in every situation because it is actually quite simple to detect. Basically, anything pushing you to do something against the Word of God is compromise—simple as that!

The three Hebrews boys enjoyed divine promotion in Babylon because of Daniel's ability to discern dreams. *"Then Daniel requested of the king, and he set Shadrach, Meshach, and Abednego, over the affairs of the province of Babylon: but Daniel sat in the gate of the king"* (Dan. 2:49, KJV). They held influential political positions, making money and living large, yet they did not allow these things or the king's influence to cause them to compromise. They knew their positions did not come from a man, but from God Almighty. They were ready to lose all for the glory of God—not only their jobs, but also their very lives.

Your obedience to God is more important than your job, career, friends, and relationships because it is obedience to God that qualifies you for the blessing. In the New Testament, the Bible says if a man loves his life, he will lose it, but if he loses it for Christ, he will find it (Matt. 10:39). Sadly, I've seen people compromising and bending rules just to advance their careers or protect their own interests. This is exactly what the enemy wants. He wants you to compromise your faith, your family, your children, and your own identity; and when you do, the spirit of compromise will always lead you into a life of double identity. When you are in church, everybody knows you as a great believer, but once you step out of the church, you are known as a great sinner. Compromising is what brings you into this place of inconsistency.

PEOPLE IN THE BIBLE WHO REFUSED TO COMPROMISE

Jesus

Matthew 4:3–10 shows us how Jesus steadfastly refused any compromise in His life:

Now when the tempter came to Him, he said, "If You are the Son of God, command that these stones become bread."

But He answered and said, "It is written, 'Man shall not live by bread alone, but by every word that proceeds from the mouth of God.' "

Then the devil took Him up into the holy city, set Him on the pinnacle of the temple, and said to Him, "If You are the Son of

God, throw Yourself down. For it is written: 'He shall give His angels charge over you,' and, 'In their hands they shall bear you up, lest you dash your foot against a stone.' "

Jesus said to him, "It is written again, 'You shall not tempt the Lord your God.' "

Again, the devil took Him up on an exceedingly high mountain, and showed Him all the kingdoms of the world and their glory. And he said to Him, "All these things I will give You if You will fall down and worship me."

Then Jesus said to him, "Away with you, Satan! For it is written, 'You shall worship the Lord your God, and Him only you shall serve.' "

Jesus did not feel He had anything to prove, because He knew His position. There was nothing He needed to do to prove his sonship. Beloved, there is nothing the devil can offer you that is better than what God has already given you.

The body of Christ today is falling into the snare of the enemy by accepting anything in the name of respecting people's freedom. We have bent the Word of God to accept gay preachers, celebrate gay marriages, and believe all kinds of lies from the devil.

Wake up, church! We are ambassadors of the kingdom of God, and as such, our responsibility is to protect the interests of the kingdom and advance its cause in the areas in which we operate. At all costs, we need to stand for righteousness, even if our lives are at stake. But when we have had an encounter with God, experienced His power and His deliverance in our lives, then we will stand firm, knowing our Redeemer lives.

Paul

Galatians 1:10–12 in the Amplified translation reads:

Now am I trying to win the favor of men, or of God? Do I seek to please men? If I were still seeking popularity with men, I should not be a bond servant of Christ (the Messiah). For I want you to know, brethren, that the Gospel which was proclaimed and made known by me is not man's gospel [a human invention, according to or patterned after any human standard]. For indeed I did not receive it from man, nor was I taught it, but [it came to me] through a [direct] revelation [given] by Jesus Christ (the Messiah).

Paul was confronted with a serious problem in the Galatian church. He had preached the gospel to them as it had been revealed to him by the Lord Jesus Christ. But then some false teachers arose, preaching a different gospel to the Galatians and gaining popularity and applause in the process. They were probably preaching a feel-good message that was filling up the pews, since that is the kind of message many people like. This placed Paul in a tough position: should he bend the gospel to accommodate everybody and make the people feel good, or should he preach the revelation he had received from the Lord? Paul refused to compromise the gospel.

It's sad to say, but in our current generation many preachers have compromised the gospel and the mandate they received from God in order to make people feel good and bolster their church membership. But these are the days of Elijah. We cannot afford to compromise and thus miss our mark. We have to stand for what we believe in, and we have to believe in what we are standing for.

THE DANGERS OF COMPROMISE

You Let God Down

Peter promised Jesus he would stand with Him and not run away. Nevertheless, when the time to stand came, Peter fell flat. Mark 14:28–31 records his sad failure:

"But after I have been raised, I will go before you to Galilee."

Peter said to Him, "Even if all are made to stumble, yet I will not be."

Jesus said to him, "Assuredly, I say to you that today, even this night, before the rooster crows twice, you will deny Me three times."

But he spoke more vehemently, "If I have to die with You, I will not deny You!" And they all said likewise.

Verse 31 in the passage above says that *"they all said likewise."* They all promised not to abandon Jesus, but when the context changed and the pressure mounted, they bent the rules and compromised on their bold declaration.

Oftentimes we act just like Peter. We make bold statements and promises to God in our prayer closets and hearts; or when we are with people who agree with us and adhere to our beliefs, we make sweeping statements of uncompromising faith. But when the chips are down, we fail to follow through with our actions. Every time we do this, we let Jesus down. In essence, we are saying, "Lord, I love You, but I don't love You enough to sacrifice my reputation, my career, my finances, or my life." But brothers and sisters, let's stand for Jesus because He stood up for us until the end!

You Become Defensive

Mark 14:66–71 reveals another aspect involved in compromise:

Now as Peter was below in the courtyard, one of the servant girls of the high priest came. And when she saw Peter warming himself, she looked at him and said, "You also were with Jesus of Nazareth."

But he denied it, saying, "I neither know nor understand what you are saying." And he went out on the porch, and a rooster crowed.

And the servant girl saw him again, and began to say to those who stood by, "This is one of them." But he denied it again.

And a little later those who stood by said to Peter again, "Surely you are one of them; for you are a Galilean, and your speech shows it."

Then he began to curse and swear, "I do not know this Man of whom you speak!"

Peter compromised first because of his physical location; the Bible says he was amidst the enemies of Jesus. Sometimes we set ourselves up to compromise by hanging around people we have no business being with or by going to places we shouldn't be going.

When a servant girl referred to Peter as one of Jesus' disciples, he first denied it by claiming he didn't understand what she was saying. The second time, he denied her claim again. But the third time, when those around him said he talked like a Galilean, Peter not only denied Jesus again but also began to curse and swear. He tried to change the way he spoke to prove that he didn't know Jesus and had nothing to do with Him. Isn't it sad that it is sometimes difficult to recognize believers outside of church because their vocabulary does not spell sanctification, the fear of God, or compassion?

Like Peter, we often become defensive because we so badly want to fit in and avoid uncomfortable situations. We are ashamed to proclaim we are Christians. But when we begin to compromise, God will always warn us, as he did in the case of Peter. The rooster crowed to warn Peter and remind him of Jesus' words, but unfortunately, Peter did not pay attention. When we do something that grieves the Holy Spirit, He will always give us an inner check in our spirits. Yet most of the time, in the heat of the moment, we try to ignore this sweet voice within.

BE ENCOURAGED

I would like to take a few moments to encourage those of you who are going through tough times. You may feel like giving up, and the devil may be offering you many shortcuts, but I pray you will take courage in the Lord your God and hold on to His Word, for after a little while, the Lord will deliver you. Do not give in, and do not compromise. Stand against the evil one, and after you have done all, stand!

Isaiah 33:15–16 gives a promise to hold on to when tempted to compromise: *"He who walks righteously and speaks uprightly, who despises gain from fraud and from oppression, who shakes his hand free from the taking of bribes, who stops his ears from hearing of bloodshed and shuts his eyes to avoid looking upon evil: he will dwell on the heights; his place of defense will be the fortress of rocks; his bread will be given him; water for him will be sure."*

This passage debunks the lies of the enemy that if you don't compromise, you'll never get ahead and succeed in life. In His Word, God has promised that if you will stand for righteousness and holiness, you will dwell among the greats and God Himself will be your provider and sustainer.

CHAPTER 6
Never Alone

Then King Nebuchadnezzar was astonished; and he rose in haste and spoke, saying to his counselors, "Did we not cast three men bound into the midst of the fire?"

They answered and said to the king, "True, O king."
"Look!" he answered, "I see four men loose, walking in the midst of the fire; and they are not hurt, and the form of the fourth is like the Son of God."

Then Nebuchadnezzar went near the mouth of the burning fiery furnace and spoke, saying, "Shadrach, Meshach, and Abed-Nego, servants of the Most High God, come out, and come here." Then Shadrach, Meshach, and Abed-Nego came from the midst of the fire.
—Daniel 3:24–26

Whenever the enemy realizes that you will not compromise, he will always try to bring persecution and trials. The Scriptures say that after the three Hebrews boys refused to bow to the carved image, the king grew very angry and commanded that the furnace be heated seven times hotter than usual. He then ordered the mighty men, the best he had, to throw the Hebrews into the fire.

Have you ever wondered why after you believed in Christ,

after you stood up for Him and witnessed to His power and might, your trials and tests seemed to suddenly intensify? The answer lies in the fact that the enemy always grows very angry with Christians who refuse to bow to the world's system. They become his main target, and he assigns his best agents to their cases. Remember, the enemy always tries to break us by applying pressure, but we can take encouragement from knowing that in the Bible, any person who stood up for righteousness faced trials.

The Bible declares that Shadrach, Meshach, and Abednego were tied up and thrown into the fire facedown. After this, the king noticed something unusual and said to his counselors, "Lo, I see four people loose and walking, and the fourth one is like the Son of God."

Right in the midst of their trial, Jesus showed up. He let them know that though they walked in the valley of the shadow of death, He was with them. No matter what we are going through, this should be our greatest comfort too, knowing that God is still on our side and will never let our feet slip.

While in the furnace, the Hebrew boys were walking. In other words, they were making progress even in the midst of their challenge. Beloved, it is possible to move forward, advance, and progress in the midst of your challenges. You have someone with you who has walked that path before, and His name is Jesus.

In the book of Acts, the Bible talks about the first Christians who stood up for what they believed in, even to the point of death. Stephen, the church's first martyr, died standing up for Christ. There is sweet inspiration in Stephen's story, so let's take a look at it:

When they heard these things they were cut to the heart, and they gnashed at him with their teeth. But he, being full of the Holy Spirit, gazed into heaven and saw the glory of God, and Jesus standing at the right hand of God, and said, "Look! I see the heavens opened and the Son of Man standing at the right hand of God!"

Then they cried out with a loud voice, stopped their ears, and ran at him with one accord; and they cast him out of the city and stoned him. And the witnesses laid down their clothes at the feet of a young man named Saul. And they stoned Stephen as he was calling on God and saying, "Lord Jesus, receive my spirit." Then he knelt down and cried out with a loud voice, "Lord, do not charge them with this sin." And when he had said this, he fell asleep.

—Acts 7:54–60

As Stephen was being stoned, he lifted his eyes to heaven and saw Jesus standing there. Interestingly, no other instance in the Bible speaks of Jesus standing; He is generally described as sitting at the right hand of the Father. But in the case of Stephen, Jesus was standing, making the statement that He is intimately involved in all our trials. When we stand for Him, He will stand for us. Please notice also that Scripture does not say Stephen died, but rather, it says he fell asleep.

We are so blessed in America to enjoy freedom of religion, but in certain parts of the world, persecution still rages and fellow believers take a stand for Christ at the risk of death. Although I always believe God will see me through every trial, I'm also mature enough to realize that taking a stand for righteousness is always costly and, truth be told, sometimes comes at the expense of our own lives.

People are always quick to criticize when someone faces challenges. However, I have come to realize that the challenges in life are not always the result of sin. Neither are we alone in any challenge. When the prophet Elijah grew discouraged and wanted to give up, he lamented his belief that he was the only prophet left and Jezebel was coming after him too. However, God reminded him that he was not alone; there were four hundred other prophets who had not bowed to Baal.

Like the disciples in the boat, sometimes we are exactly where Jesus wants us to be but still experience storms. Nevertheless, I have good news for you: you are never alone in the midst of your situation, sickness, trial, or test. The enemy will try to persuade you that you are alone and forsaken, whispering that all your friends have left you, your family does not understand what you are going through, or nobody wants to identify with you. Even so, don't buy into his lies. Just as Jesus was aboard the boat with His disciples, He is with you in the midst of every situation.

I would rather have God's approval and backing than have the crowd clapping wildly for me. God on your side is better than anything you could ever dream of having. He is the Creator of heaven and earth, He moves things by the power of His word, and kings seek wisdom at His feet. His name has influence in heaven, on earth, and under the earth, and as His child, you have the benefit of that name to sustain you through every trial.

CHAPTER 7
A New Generation

Let's start this chapter by reading 1 Samuel 16:1–13:
Now the LORD said to Samuel, "How long will you mourn for Saul, seeing I have rejected him from reigning over Israel? Fill your horn with oil, and go; I am sending you to Jesse the Bethlehemite. For I have provided Myself a king among his sons."

And Samuel said, "How can I go? If Saul hears it, he will kill me."

But the LORD said, "Take a heifer with you, and say, 'I have come to sacrifice to the LORD.' Then invite Jesse to the sacrifice, and I will show you what you shall do; you shall anoint for Me the one I name to you."

So Samuel did what the LORD said, and went to Bethlehem. And the elders of the town trembled at his coming, and said, "Do you come peaceably?"

And he said, "Peaceably; I have come to sacrifice to the LORD. Sanctify yourselves, and come with me to the sacrifice." Then he consecrated Jesse and his sons, and invited them to the sacrifice.

So it was, when they came, that he looked at Eliab and said,

"Surely the LORD's anointed is before Him!"

But the LORD said to Samuel, "Do not look at his appearance or at his physical stature, because I have refused him. For the LORD does not see as man sees; for man looks at the outward appearance, but the LORD looks at the heart."

So Jesse called Abinadab, and made him pass before Samuel. And he said, "Neither has the LORD chosen this one." Then Jesse made Shammah pass by. And he said, "Neither has the LORD chosen this one." Thus Jesse made seven of his sons pass before Samuel. And Samuel said to Jesse, "The LORD has not chosen these." And Samuel said to Jesse, "Are all the young men here?" Then he said, "There remains yet the youngest, and there he is, keeping the sheep."

And Samuel said to Jesse, "Send and bring him. For we will not sit down till he comes here." So he sent and brought him in. Now he was ruddy, with bright eyes, and good-looking. And the LORD said, "Arise, anoint him; for this is the one!" Then Samuel took the horn of oil and anointed him in the midst of his brothers; and the Spirit of the LORD came upon David from that day forward. So Samuel arose and went to Ramah.

Saul had been elected king by the people of Israel because of his appearance. The Bible states there was no one taller than Saul in all of Israel (1 Sam. 10:23–24). Yet God later rejected Saul because of his disobedience to a divine command. Having been elected by the people, Saul acted to please the people. That's because whatever elects you will always direct you.

I see this same pattern in the church today. Pastors who were hired by a board are sometimes led by their members. I don't take issue with having a church board, but I don't believe the board should dictate the vision of the church. Only the pastor should do that. As a friend of mine always says, God will never leave the head to talk to the leg or the arm.

In 1 Samuel 16:1, God asked a question of the prophet Samuel: "How long will you mourn for Saul?" Saul represents the past, something that has been done away with. It is over, and it's time on God's calendar has expired. But Samuel was still mourning Saul, the first king of Israel, the man who bore the outward appearance of a king but lacked the interior qualities of true leadership. Frequently we act just like Samuel and cry for those things God has rejected, things He has removed from His agenda because He knows we deserve better. At times we cry because we don't believe there is anything better than what we have lost, but like Samuel, we cannot afford to be fooled by appearances.

When God told Samuel to go to Jesse's house, Samuel already had his mind set on how the next king should look, walk, and talk. When he saw Eliab, the firstborn of Jesse, the one who represented the identity, the honor, and the dignity of the family, he therefore assumed he must be the one. The Bible describes Eliab as being tall and built like a man of war; when Samuel saw him, he was probably reminded of Saul.

Many times in our lives, we, too, judge by appearance. Trying desperately to cover our losses, we jump on anything that looks like what we have lost. I will admit, even men of God occasionally make this mistake. Samuel, for instance, was one of the greatest prophets in Israel, yet he almost anointed Eliab king of Israel. God had to step in and tell him to wait. He couldn't allow Samuel to select a king for His people based on fleshly perception. As far as God was concerned, the criteria for selection had shifted. Samuel had anointed Saul based on the people's choice, and therefore on the flesh, but this time the selection was to be based on God's choice. His only criterion then—as it is now in this end-time generation—was the condition of the heart.

Because of this tendency to judge by appearances, many men of God today struggle to accept what God is doing in their ministries. Please listen to me, church leaders. What God is doing in this season has nothing to do with theology, denomination, or the like. If you are still looking for the move of God through the eyes of a denomination, background, or theology, you will miss it.

I am not downgrading education or the importance of training; all I'm saying is God is doing something much bigger than an education or a denomination. The people God is using in your ministry may not fit your idea of typical men and women of God, but unless you exchange your eyes for God's, you might stand as a barrier to the move of God. Remember, men promote talent, abilities, and achievements, but God promotes character.

God chose David because he was a man after God's own heart. Our resemblance to God is not a resemblance of face, accent, or skin color; our resemblance is based on the attitude of the heart. The image of God must be reflected in the image of the heart. As I often say, character is our responsibility and the anointing is God's.

Seven of Jesse's sons stood before Samuel. The number seven in the Bible signifies perfection or completion. In one sense, these seven sons pictured the perfection of the flesh, as Jesse perceived it. He presented all the sons he thought were qualified to become the next king of Israel. Since the prophet did not sense a release in his spirit to anoint any of them, he asked Jesse if he had any other sons. I don't imagine for a second that Jesse had forgotten he had another son in the field, but he overlooked him because he was the youngest and seemed the most unlikely candidate. Sometimes it is like that: the person we despise or value lightly is the one that God has His eyes on.

David did not look like any of his brothers. He was not built as a man of war, and neither did he have the stature of a king. The Bible describes him as a ruddy young man with a pretty face. However, he was God's choice. You see, David was the eighth child of Jesse, and the number eight stands for a new beginning.

I believe God is raising up a new generation today and ushering in a new beginning that will bring Christ back to the earth. In this end-time generation, God is using people who may not speak, talk, or act like what we are accustomed to. But that does not mean they are not from God.

We need a David generation, a generation of people passionate about pleasing God and Him alone. These are people who worship in a way that brings God on the scene and overcomes evil spirits, people who understand God's power and are not afraid to boldly challenge any Goliath, people who need no title to do the work of their God.

God's criteria for selection are much different from man's. This is quite clear in 1 Corinthians 1:26–29:

For you see your calling, brethren, that not many wise according to the flesh, not many mighty, not many noble, are called. But God has chosen the foolish things of the world to put to shame the wise, and God has chosen the weak things of the world to put to shame the things which are mighty; and the base things of the world and the things which are despised God has chosen, and the things which are not, to bring to nothing the things that are, that no flesh should glory in His presence.

God chooses the least of society, the rejected of our system, the despised of our world, and the weakest among us and uses them in His kingdom and for His purpose. Paul says the reason God does this is so that no flesh can glory in His presence. You cannot receive the glory when you realize that everything you do is by His grace and mercy alone.

CHAPTER 8
You Are Unbreakable

One of the goals of the enemy is to break the resolve and effectiveness of this generation that God is raising up. The way he does it is by applying pressure on our lives so that we give in and break. In 2 Corinthians 4:7–10, however, Paul reminds us that we are carriers of something so precious, valuable, rare, and peculiar that nothing can overcome it. The passage reads: "But we have this treasure in earthen vessels, that the excellence of the power may be of God and not of us. We are hard-pressed on every side, yet not crushed; we are perplexed, but not in despair; persecuted, but not forsaken; struck down, but not destroyed—always carrying about in the body the dying of the Lord Jesus, that the life of Jesus also may be manifested in our body." What is this treasure God has deposited inside each and every one of us? It is Jesus Himself—the Word dwelling within us!

According to John 1:1–5, the Word has existed from the beginning, and nothing that was created came into being without Him: *"In the beginning was the Word, and the Word was with God, and the Word was God. He was in the beginning with God. All things were made through Him, and without Him nothing was made that was made. In Him was life, and the life was the light of men. And the light shines in the darkness, and the darkness did not comprehend it."*

God has taken His secret creative formula and deposited it inside of you. That substance, called the Word, was used to created the heavens and the earth, and it has been placed on the inside of you. What a privilege to be a carrier of God's divine substance of creation!

Paul said that we are the temple of God: *"You are the temple of the living God. As God has said: 'I will dwell in them and walk among them. I will be their God, and they shall be My people'"* (2 Cor. 6:16). Also, we read in 1 Corinthians 3:16, *"Do you not know that you are the temple of God and that the Spirit of God dwells in you?*

We are the dwelling place of God, and His presence is the treasure we carry on the inside of us. The devil has no creative power or ability and thus seeks that creative substance within us called the Word. If he can gain access to it, he can use it to foster his agenda in this generation; when we guard it, however, we create a climate that fosters the agenda of the kingdom of God.

God has made us vessels of that Word, and because of the treasure we carry, we are the battleground for the enemy's attacks. Paul reminds us that is why we face so many trials. But the enemy is not after every Christian, only those who are actual carriers of the Word of God. Until the Word is dwelling richly in us, we'll never be a target for the enemy.

To those of you who are facing a great trial and don't understand why, I encourage you that maybe it is because you are a vessel of God's Word. Maybe it's because you are a carrier of the power to heal the sick, deliver the captives, and release communities and nations. Jacob had twelve sons, all of them seeds of Abraham, yet it was Joseph who experienced the greatest struggles. Why? Because Joseph was the carrier of the prophetic word. Perhaps that is the case in your life too.

YOU ARE THE BATTLEGROUND

Once you understand that as a carrier of this treasure, you are automatically on the devil's A list, you will be better prepared when he launches his attack to gain access to the treasure. But never forget that "no weapon formed against you shall prosper" (Isa. 54:17). Weapons, of course, are designed for attack, but the Bible is saying that though the enemy will indeed attack and try to break you, he will not be able to succeed in the attempt. The enemy will assault your life, your health, your finances, and your marriage, but the Bible says his attack will not prosper.

God will always cause us to triumph in every attack and battle: "Now thanks be unto God, which always causeth us to triumph in Christ, and maketh manifest the savour of his knowledge by us in every place" (2 Cor. 2:14, KJV). Since that is true, God expects you to win every battle that the enemy brings your way.

You are made of a material stronger and more resilient than anything in the world. The God on the inside of you is stronger than anything the enemy can throw at you. "You are of God, little children, and have overcome them, because He who is in you is greater than he who is in the world" (1 John 4:4).

THE DEVIL S STRATEGIES OF ATTACK

In the passage from 2 Corinthians 4, Paul outlines four main strategies the enemy uses to apply pressure:

1. **He tries to hard-press you.**

If you are hard-pressed, you are experiencing great difficulties, with your back against the wall. Beloved, the enemy will try to hard-press you on every side to see if you will break under pressure. You might find your marriage pressed, your finances pressed, your career pressed, and you might even experience all these at the same time. Your attitude in the midst of the pressure will determine whether you'll give in and break or whether you will resist and persevere.

Paul said that even though he was pressed on every side, he refused to be crushed. The word crush means to subdue, to bring low in condition, or to break. You have to make up your mind that you'll not be crushed or have a nervous breakdown in the midst of trial, no matter how intense the pressure.

2. He tries to perplex you.

To be perplexed means to be confused or puzzled. Sometimes we become confused when the enemy attacks on every front of the battle, and we start wondering whether we are in the will of God or whether God has forgotten about us. In the fight to preserve this treasure on the inside of us, we might become confused about what we are going through, but we need to remember one thing: we cannot afford to break

Never give in to despair, no matter how confusing the situation. To despair is to lose all hope and confidence. That's what the enemy wants you to do when he brings confusion into your marriage, your ministry, your finances, your health, or your business. He wants you to lose hope and break. But that's exactly the time when you need to tap into the treasure on the inside of you and let it build a layer of strength in your mind.

3. He tries to persecute you.

To persecute someone means to harass, to oppress, or to persistently annoy that person. There will be times in your Christian life when the enemy will annoy you consistently and harass your life, your relationships, your future, or your family; but in those times, you have to make up your mind not to give up or abandon hope. Remember, there is a treasure on the inside of you.

4. He tries to strike you down.

To strike something down means to incapacitate it or render it ineffective. The enemy will try to nullify your work, to render you ineffective so you cannot operate and walk in your assignment. But Paul said that we are not destroyed. In other words, you cannot be broken or demolished.

CHAPTER 9
The Spirit Upon

Throughout church history, disagreement about the manifestation and impartation of the Holy Spirit has always existed. We have seen the manifestation of all three persons of the trinity, God the Father, God the Son, and God the Holy Spirit.

In the book of Genesis, we find God introducing Jesus, the seed of the woman, who would crush the head of the enemy: *"And I will put enmity between you and the woman, and between your seed and her Seed; He shall bruise your head, and you shall bruise His heel"* (Gen. 3:15).

In the New Testament, Jesus announced to His disciples the coming of the Holy Spirit: *"But this He spoke concerning the Spirit, whom those believing in Him would receive; for the Holy Spirit was not yet given, because Jesus was not yet glorified"* (John 7:39). Earlier in that chapter, Jesus said it was imperative for Him to leave. You might wonder why He would say that.

I believe Jesus, as a human being, was restricted in His ability to reach the whole world. Though He was fully God, He was still fully man. Consequently, He was limited by natural laws. He couldn't be everywhere at the same time. Heaven needed a strategy to reach the whole world with the same message and the same power that Jesus carried on earth. The most effective way to accomplish this was through the ministry of the Holy Spirit.

The Holy Spirit is omnipresent, meaning He is in all places at all times. The Holy Spirit is manifested in two forms in our lives: the Spirit within us and the Spirit upon us.

THE SPIRIT WITHIN US

We receive the Holy Spirit within us when we accept Jesus as our Lord and Savior. It is this form of the Spirit that enables us to identify with God as Father. As Romans 8:14–16 explains, *"For as many as are led by the Spirit of God, these are sons of God. For you did not receive the spirit of bondage again to fear, but you received the Spirit of adoption by whom we cry out, 'Abba, Father.' The Spirit Himself bears witness with our spirit that we are children of God."*

When we are born again, we receive the "within" Spirit. This form of the Spirit is responsible for developing our character in order to reflect the image of Jesus Christ. The result of the Spirit within is the fruit of the Spirit: *"But the fruit of the Spirit is love, joy, peace, longsuffering, kindness, goodness, faithfulness, gentleness, self-control. Against such there is no law. And those who are Christ's have crucified the flesh with its passions and desires"* (Gal. 5:22–24). Every believer is called to demonstrate the fruit of the Spirit as evidence of a new life in Christ.

In John 20:21–23, Jesus breathed on His disciples and said, *"Receive the Holy Spirit,"* not *"You will receive the Holy Spirit."* The Amplified Bible records it like this: *"Then Jesus said to them again, Peace to you! [Just] as the Father has sent Me forth, so I am sending you. And having said this, He breathed on them and said to them, Receive the Holy Spirit! [Now having received the Holy Spirit, and being led and directed by Him] if you forgive the sins of anyone, they are forgiven; if you retain the sins of anyone, they are retained."* This implies that the disciples received the Holy Spirit as soon as Jesus spoke the words. The Bible does not say they began prophesying or speaking in new tongues, because what they received at that moment was the Spirit within, not the Spirit upon.

Later Jesus spoke to these same disciples and told them to wait for the Holy Spirit: "And being assembled together with them, He commanded them not to depart from Jerusalem, but to wait for the Promise of the Father, 'which,' He said, 'you have heard from Me; for John truly baptized with water, but you shall be baptized with the Holy Spirit not many days from now' " (Acts 1:4–5).

You might wonder why Jesus would tell His disciples to wait for the Spirit if they had already received the Spirit when He breathed on them. In telling His disciples to wait for the Spirit, Jesus was making a distinction between the Spirit that was already within them and the Spirit that was yet to come upon them.

THE SPIRIT UPON US

When Jesus told the disciples to tarry until the promise came, He was referring to the power of the Holy Spirit, which is the Spirit upon us. Acts 1:4–8 records:

And being assembled together with them, He commanded them not to depart from Jerusalem, but to wait for the Promise of the Father, "which," He said, "you have heard from Me; for John truly baptized with water, but you shall be baptized with the Holy Spirit not many days from now." Therefore, when they had come together, they asked Him, saying, "Lord, will You at this time restore the kingdom to Israel?" And He said to them, "It is not for you to know times or seasons which the Father has put in His own authority. But you shall receive power when the Holy Spirit has come upon you; and you shall be witnesses to Me in Jerusalem, and in all Judea and Samaria, and to the end of the earth."

In the Old Testament, the Spirit came upon people to enable them to do the work of God. They did not have the privilege of receiving the Spirit within them, because the blood of Jesus had not yet been shed on the cross. Therefore, they could not refer to God as Father because it is the Spirit within us that causes us to cry "Abba Father." But now, since the blood of Jesus has been shed, we have the privilege of receiving the Spirit within and can be called sons and daughters of God.

Nevertheless, the truth and reality about the Spirit upon is similar to the Old Testament experiences. The Spirit upon is sometimes referred to as the "anointing" of God. It is the ability to perform the supernatural in the natural realm. It is that which empowers us to do things we could never do in our own strength.

This form of the Spirit is what the Bible talks about in the book of Acts, and it is introduced in the second chapter: *"When the Day of Pentecost had fully come, they were all with one accord in one place. And suddenly there came a sound from heaven, as of a rushing mighty wind, and it filled the whole house where they were sitting. Then there appeared to them divided tongues, as of fire, and one sat upon each of them. And they were all filled with the Holy Spirit and began to speak with other tongues, as the Spirit gave them utterance"* (Acts 2:1–4).

The disciples tarried for many days in prayer and fasting until the Holy Spirit came upon them. When the Spirit was released upon them, Peter, who had denied Jesus three times, suddenly received supernatural power to witness about the same Jesus to more than three thousand people. The same disciples who had been unable to cast a demon from a child now received supernatural power to heal the sick, cast out demons, and raise the dead. The Spirit upon has the ability to take regular men and women and transform them into demon busters, city shakers, community transformers, and nation movers.

In the book of 1 Samuel, the Bible makes reference to the fact that when the Spirit of the Lord came upon Saul, he became a different man.

> *"Then the Spirit of the LORD will come upon you, and you will prophesy with them and be turned into another man. And let it be, when these signs come to you, that you do as the occasion demands; for God is with you. You shall go down before me to Gilgal; and surely I will come down to you to offer burnt offerings and make sacrifices of peace offerings. Seven days you shall wait, till I come to you and show you what you should do."*
>
> *So it was, when he had turned his back to go from Samuel, that God gave him another heart; and all those signs came to pass that day. When they came there to the hill, there was a group of prophets to meet him; then the Spirit of God came upon him, and he prophesied among them.*
>
> —1 Samuel 10:6–10

Something supernatural happens once the Holy Spirit lays hold of us. We become a very real threat to the devil when we walk in the power of the Spirit of God. The devil knows this, but unfortunately, he has deceived many Christians about the power they have when the Spirit comes upon them.

Though a free gift from God, the Spirit upon (the anointing) requires a personal level of consecration in order to be manifested in our lives. Jesus told the disciples to tarry and wait until the promise came. The Bible makes it clear they spent many days fasting and praying in the upper room. This means they consecrated themselves and denied themselves in order to activate the promise of the Spirit.

I have read stories of great men of God who walked under a mighty influence of the Spirit, and behind all the power and the anointing was a high level of discipline and consecration. Few

Christians today, however, walk in such power of the Spirit because few are willing to pay the price.

Some denominations, emphasizing the Spirit within, consider the manifestation of the Spirit's power as outdated, since they lack the willingness to go further and to pay the price. But if we are ever going to affect this world as Jesus did, we need the combination of the Spirit within and the Spirit upon. By the Spirit within, we help the oppressed, and by the spirit upon, we deliver the oppressed.

The Spirit upon produces the gifts of the Spirit. These gifts are also referred to as "signs and wonders." Signs indicate a particular direction. In the days and times in which we live, people need to see signs that point in the right direction. One way we provide this is by having an encounter with and then a manifestation of the Spirit's power.

When John the Baptist wondered if Jesus was the Messiah, he sent his disciples to ask whether He was the one or whether he should wait for another. Jesus did not respond by declaring "I am the one," but rather, He pointed to the signs that proved He was the promised Messiah:

When the men came to Jesus, they said, "John the Baptist sent us to you to ask, 'Are you the one who is to come, or should we expect someone else?'"

At that very time Jesus cured many who had diseases, sicknesses and evil spirits, and gave sight to many who were blind. 22. So he replied to the messengers, "Go back and report to John what you have seen and heard: The blind receive sight, the lame walk, those who have leprosy[a] are cleansed, the deaf hear, the dead are raised, and the good news is proclaimed to the poor.

–Luke 7:20-22

Many people today are asking the same question: "Is Jesus the real deal, or should we seek another?" The only way to convince them of Jesus' identity is by pointing them to the manifestation of the Holy Spirit in signs and wonders.

I remember once when I was young, my sister and I were watching This Is Your Day with Benny Hinn. During the show, he stretched his hands toward the camera and asked the viewers to put their hands on the television screen for the power of God to touch them. I was very naive and curious and decided to touch the screen to see if anything would happen. When I did, I sensed power going through my hands, and I was projected about two feet from where I was standing. From that moment on, I have known that the power of God is real and that Jesus is real.

One encounter with the power of God can change a person's life. It is amazing, though, how many unbelievers come into our churches and leave the same way they came in because there is no manifestation of the Spirit upon. People tend to believe their problems are bigger than anyone else's, and often they will not submit to anything else unless they experience a power greater than their problems. It is crucial, therefore, for the Spirit upon to be evident in every believer's life. Remember, Jesus didn't impact His generation with great speeches or by His pedigree, but through the Spirit upon.

Jesus waited thirty years before receiving the Spirit upon to start His ministry. In Luke 4:18–19, He read from the book of Isaiah, making clear the intent and scope of His ministry: *"And when He had opened the book, He found the place where it was written: 'The Spirit of the LORD is upon Me, because He has anointed Me to preach the gospel to the poor; He has sent Me to heal the brokenhearted, to proclaim liberty to the captives and recovery of sight to the blind, to set at liberty those who are oppressed; to proclaim the acceptable year of the LORD.' "*

Imagine what would happen if every believer could demonstrate the Spirit upon in his or her life. Like the apostles who turned their cities upside down, we, too, would be able to drive the devil out of our cities, communities, and nations. With the Spirit upon, we could demonstrate to the powers of the occult, to the witches, wizards, and all satanic powers that exist, that there is a higher power. Until we walk in this power of the Holy Spirit, however, we will limit ourselves to debates, discussions, and reflections about faith. Never forget that the enemy does not respond to anything except the power of God.

All the great men and women in the Bible who confronted the power of the enemy walked with the Spirit upon them. The Bible tells us in the book of Acts about Simon the sorcerer, who succeeded in deceiving an entire city by the miracles he performed through the spirit of divination. However, when Philip arrived in the city and began demonstrating the power of the Spirit upon, people acknowledged the true power of God working through him. Even Simon recognized that Philip had a power different from his own:

Then Philip went down to the[a] city of Samaria and preached Christ to them. 6. And the multitudes with one accord heeded the things spoken by Philip, hearing and seeing the miracles which he did. 7. For unclean spirits, crying with a loud voice, came out of many who were possessed; and many who were paralyzed and lame were healed. 8. And there was great joy in that city.

But there was a certain man called Simon, who previously practiced sorcery in the city and astonished the people of Samaria, claiming that he was someone great, 10. to whom they all gave heed, from the least to the greatest, saying, "This man is the great power of God." 11. And they heeded him because he had astonished them with his sorceries for a long time. 12. But when they believed Philip as he preached the things concerning the kingdom of God and the name of Jesus Christ, both men and women were baptized. 13. Then Simon himself also believed; and when he was baptized he continued with Philip, and was amazed, seeing the miracles and signs which were done.

—Acts 8:5-13

CHAPTER 10
Fight or Faint

Deuteronomy 20:8–9 declares, *"The officers shall speak further to the people, and say, 'What man is there who is fearful and fainthearted? Let him go and return to his house, lest the heart of his brethren faint like his heart.' And so it shall be, when the officers have finished speaking to the people, that they shall make captains of the armies to lead the people."*

A battle is raging against our faith and the advancement of the kingdom of God. Like the Israelites of old, we must rise to the challenge and put on our armor to fight the enemy of our faith. The battle line has been drawn and the challenge issued to our kingdom and the king we represent. We cannot draw back or run away.

William Booth, the founder of the Salvation Army, in his last address in the Royal Albert Hall on 9 May 1912 said the following:

> *"While women weep, as they do now, I'll fight; while little children go hungry, as they do now, I'll fight; while men go to prison, in and out, in and out, as they do now, I'll fight; while there is a drunkard left, while there is a poor lost girl upon the streets, while there remains one dark soul without the light of God, I'll fight-I'll fight to the very end!"*

There is always a reason to fight and stand for the gospel of our Lord and Savior Jesus Christ. In the Old Testament, God's people picked up their swords and fought physical enemies. They marched into battle to conquer nations and subdue their enemies. However, in this current season, the battle has shifted. It is no longer a physical battle, but a spiritual one. As Paul said, we wrestle not against flesh and blood.

One of the ways we fight spiritually is through warfare prayer. In Luke 18:1, Jesus taught that *"men ought always to pray, and not to faint"* (KJV). To illustrate this point, Jesus shared a parable to show the disciples the necessity of persistent spiritual warfare.

Prayer is crucial for our survival as instruments in the hands of God. I cannot overemphasize our need for prayer. Prayerless people are usually the first to give up in a difficult situation. Why? Because they don't have any promises to hang onto. As Psalm 27:13 says, *"I had fainted, unless I had believed to see the goodness of the Lord in the land of the living"* (KJV).

WHY PEOPLE FAINT

There are two main reasons why people faint in the day of battle: (1) the cost and (2) weariness. Let's look at them one at a time and see what we can learn.

The Cost

The high cost of following Jesus is a major reason why many people faint and turn back from serving Him wholeheartedly. The passage below sheds much light on the topic:

And when Jesus saw great multitudes about Him, He gave a command to depart to the other side. Then a certain scribe came

> *and said to Him, "Teacher, I will follow You wherever You go."*
>
> *And Jesus said to him, "Foxes have holes and birds of the air have nests, but the Son of Man has nowhere to lay His head."*
>
> *Then another of His disciples said to Him, "Lord, let me first go and bury my father."*
>
> *But Jesus said to him, "Follow Me, and let the dead bury their own dead."*
>
> —Matthew 8:18–22

Some of us are not involved in the fight, not because the call of Christ has no appeal, but because the high cost of discipleship has no appeal. Some of us are called to be missionaries and pastors, and some of us are called to perform specific assignments in the kingdom; yet few are boldly embracing the call. When we look at everything we have to walk away from or the disapproval from others that might result from following the call, we faint.

But no cost could be greater than what the Son of God, Jesus Christ, paid on Calvary. We might be concerned about our positions, reputations, or the opinions of others, but no matter what price we are called to pay, Christ paid a much higher one to save you and me.

Weariness

Weariness in the day of battle is another reason people sometimes faint. Let's look at the story of Elijah to see this factor in operation:

> *And Ahab told Jezebel all that Elijah had done, also how he had executed all the prophets with the sword. Then Jezebel sent a messenger to Elijah, saying, "So let the gods do to me, and*

more also, if I do not make your life as the life of one of them by tomorrow about this time." And when he saw that, he arose and ran for his life, and went to Beersheba, which belongs to Judah, and left his servant there.

But he himself went a day's journey into the wilderness, and came and sat down under a broom tree. And he prayed that he might die, and said, "It is enough! Now, LORD, take my life, for I am no better than my fathers!"

Then as he lay and slept under a broom tree, suddenly an angel touched him, and said to him, "Arise and eat." Then he looked, and there by his head was a cake baked on coals, and a jar of water. So he ate and drank, and lay down again. And the angel of the LORD came back the second time, and touched him, and said, "Arise and eat, because the journey is too great for you." So he arose, and ate and drank; and he went in the strength of that food forty days and forty nights as far as Horeb, the mountain of God.

And there he went into a cave, and spent the night in that place; and behold, the word of the LORD came to him, and He said to him, "What are you doing here, Elijah?"

So he said, "I have been very zealous for the LORD God of hosts; for the children of Israel have forsaken Your covenant, torn down Your altars, and killed Your prophets with the sword. I alone am left; and they seek to take my life."
—1 Kings 19:1–10

After Elijah's victory at Mount Carmel, he received a message in which Jezebel basically declared war against him. In verse 10, God confronted Elijah, asking him,

"What are you doing here, Elijah?" In other words, God was saying, "I was not expecting you to be hiding in a cave, Elijah.

My name is being defied, and I thought you would take your position and fight."

But Elijah was weary and thought all his work had been in vain. The people were still forsaking the covenant, and he felt alone. Occasionally in life, when the battles seem to intensify by the hour, we are ready to throw in the towel because we think that all the sacrifices we have made have not yielded any fruit. Such thinking is symptomatic of weariness and an indication of discouragement. In those times, we lose hope for the very things we have been fighting for and believing God for.

The Bible says if we faint in the day of trouble, our strength is weak (Prov. 24:10). Nevertheless, many people in the body of Christ faint quickly at the slightest hint of mounting pressure and opposition. But we will never know what we are made of until pressure and adversity begin to push us down. That is the time for our spiritual strength to arise. And remember, the word strength means the power to resist strain, stress, or attack; it implies impregnability against any obstacle.

So how can we get strength to fight? Isaiah 40:29 provides the answer: "He gives power to the weak, and to those who have no might He increases strength." God gives us power and increases our strength when we feel weak. He does it through the medium of prayer. I have said it before, and I need to emphasize again, that many Christians become weary because of their lack of prayer. If there is no prayer, there is no power and no strength.

WHAT TO DO WHEN YOU FEEL LIKE FAINTING

When you feel like fainting, you can take various actions to keep yourself on track. However, as I have looked through the pages of the Bible, I believe these can be summed up in the word believe. Despite the gravity of the situation you face, you must be convinced that God will come through for you. Believing is the antidote to fainting.

There are three main things you must believe in: prayer, the promises of God, and His church on earth. Let's look now at these vital aspects of persevering in the day of battle.

Believe in Prayer

Jonah 2:7 says, *"When my soul fainted within me, I remembered the LORD; and my prayer went up to You, into Your holy temple."* Lack of prayer is the number one reason people faint, but those who pray possess a strength that prayerless people will never experience. However, it is not enough to say that you believe in prayer; you must demonstrate your belief by actually praying. Prayer, then, is the first part of the antidote to fainting.

Another verse that encourages prayer is Psalm 27:14: *"Wait on the Lord; be of good courage, and He shall strengthen thine heart; wait, I say, on the Lord"* (KJV). Isaiah 40:31 is similar: *"But those who wait on the LORD shall renew their strength; they shall mount up with wings like eagles, they shall run and not be weary, they shall walk and not faint."* The waiting season should be dedicated to prayer and intercession. As a spiritual exercise, prayer will strengthen your spiritual muscles and build your spiritual tenacity, but unless you actually pray, you can reap no benefit from its potential power.

Remember, Jesus declared that *"men ought always to pray, and not to faint"* (Luke 18:1, KJV). He obviously did not believe praying and fainting could reside in the same heart at the same time. When we read the passage in Luke 18, we realize that Jesus is not talking about a one-time prayer or a quick-fix prayer, but He is emphasizing the importance of persistent prayer. In order to stand and not faint, we must develop consistent prayer lives because prayer is the weapon that will keep our hopes alive and change our situations.

In the Garden of Gethsemane, we see a clear example of how

Jesus won the battle over fainting:

> Then Jesus came with them to a place called Gethsemane, and said to the disciples, *"Sit here while I go and pray over there."* And He took with Him Peter and the two sons of Zebedee, and He began to be sorrowful and deeply distressed. Then He said to them, *"My soul is exceedingly sorrowful, even to death. Stay here and watch with Me."*
>
> He went a little farther and fell on His face, and prayed, saying, *"O My Father, if it is possible, let this cup pass from Me; nevertheless, not as I will, but as You will."*
>
> Then He came to the disciples and found them sleeping, and said to Peter, *"What! Could you not watch with Me one hour? Watch and pray, lest you enter into temptation. The spirit indeed is willing, but the flesh is weak."*
>
> Again, a second time, He went away and prayed, saying, *"O My Father, if this cup cannot pass away from Me unless I drink it, Your will be done."* And He came and found them asleep again, for their eyes were heavy.
> —Matthew 26:36–43

As Jesus envisioned His mission, He thought about everything He would have to endure and was filled with distress. Nevertheless, He gave himself to prayer. There He found the power and strength He needed to walk through His final hours. His disciples, however, did not give themselves to prayer and thus fainted in the hour of testing.

Here is another illustration of the power of prayer:
But after long abstinence from food, then Paul stood in the midst of them and said, "Men, you should have listened to me, and not have sailed from Crete and incurred this disaster and loss. And now I urge you to take heart, for there will be no loss

of life among you, but only of the ship. For there stood by me this night an angel of the God to whom I belong and whom I serve, saying, 'Do not be afraid, Paul; you must be brought before Caesar; and indeed God has granted you all those who sail with you.' Therefore take heart, men, for I believe God that it will be just as it was told me."
—Acts 27:21–25

Through the strength born of prayer, Paul refused to faint and thus saved both himself and those who sailed with him. When you stay on your knees in prayer, strength and boldness arise inside of you in times of trouble because you know the outcome of the situation you face.

Believe in the Promises of God

There is nothing more debilitating than believing you are fighting an already lost battle. Conversely, there is nothing more invigorating than the conviction that, all appearances to the contrary notwithstanding, you are sure to win. Jesus had to strengthen Himself with this conviction. For the joy that was set before Him—the joy of victory, the joy of drawing all men unto Himself—He *"endured the cross, despising the shame"* (Heb. 12:2)

Paul, too, knew the necessity of clinging to God's promises. In Galatians 6:9, he encouraged, *"And let us not be weary in well doing, for in due season we shall reap, if we faint not."* If you want to overcome the spirit of fainting, you must believe in the promises of God.

Believe in the Church

Ecclesiastes 4:9–12 speaks of the power found in joining with others in battle: *"Two are better than one, because they have a good return for their work: If one falls down, his friend can help him up. But pity the man who falls and has no one to help him up! Also, if two lie down together, they will keep warm. But how can one keep warm alone? Though one may be overpowered, two can defend themselves. A cord of three strands is not quickly broken."*

In a direct attack on this scriptural truth, the enemy often uses the strategy of isolation. Many people, when facing discouragement and feelings of fainting, begin withdrawing from the church; they sever contact with other believers and seclude themselves in their houses. But it is precisely during this season that they most need to draw close to the house of God in order to be strengthened, encouraged, and empowered to run the race.

Never underestimate the power of fellowship as you go through battles. When God's people in the Old Testament faced a battle, they called for an army. So must it be in our time. The church must come together as the army of God fighting for the same cause.

I learned early in life that the best fighters never work alone. In the army, no matter how skilled a particular soldier may be, he or she understands the crucial need for fellow soldiers to cover or back him or her up. It must be the same in the church.

God alone is the giver of strength and the one who enables us to not faint in the day of battle. As the Bible says in Isaiah 40:28–31:

Have you not known?
Have you not heard?
The everlasting God, the LORD,
The Creator of the ends of the earth,
Neither faints nor is weary.
His understanding is unsearchable.
He gives power to the weak,

*And to those who have no might He increases strength.
Even the youths shall faint and be weary,
And the young men shall utterly fall,
But those who wait on the LORD
Shall renew their strength;
They shall mount up with wings as eagles,
They shall run and not be weary,
They shall walk and not faint.*

CHAPTER 11
Finish Strong

In Philippians 3:12–16, Paul boldly asserted his plan to finish strong in the call upon his life:

Not that I have already attained, or am already perfected; but I press on, that I may lay hold of that for which Christ Jesus has also laid hold of me. Brethren, I do not count myself to have apprehended; but one thing I do, forgetting those things which are behind and reaching forward to those things which are ahead, I press toward the goal for the prize of the upward call of God in Christ Jesus.

Therefore let us, as many as are mature, have this mind; and if in anything you think otherwise, God will reveal even this to you. Nevertheless, to the degree that we have already attained, let us walk by the same rule, let us be of the same mind.

The apostle Paul is one of the spiritual giants of the New Testament. He wrote most of the New Testament and helped establish many churches all over Asia. He witnessed the power of God in tremendous ways. He also suffered betrayals, offenses, beatings, and persecutions for the sake of the gospel. He is a solid example that we can glean from as we, too, run our races. In the passage above, Paul relates to us, not only the secrets of his ministry, but also those of his personal walk with God.

Our walk with God is similar to a race, and a race is not so much about how we start, but how we finish. That is why the Bible says better the end than the beginning of a race. If a race's outcome were based solely on the beginning, most of us would be disqualified from the outset, considering our pasts, our families' backgrounds, and all the wrong steps we took along the way.

Some of us have come from broken homes, some of us have come from abusive relationships, and some of us have struggled with drug addictions. All kinds of things could seemingly disqualify us from the race. But thanks be to Christ who has qualified us in the race through the shedding of His blood on Calvary. He has given us the hope that no matter how we started in life (broke, sinner, drunkard, liar, etc.), we can finish strong. We have not arrived, but we are in the process. The race is still in motion, and we are still competing.

ACKNOWLEDGE YOUR POSITION

Before you can go to the next level in this race of life, whether in business, finances, relationship, or ministry, you must assess yourself. You need to know your weaknesses as well as your strengths.

The apostle Paul clearly acknowledged that he had not yet finished his race, but he knew his position in relation to the finish line. However, many people have a hard time being honest with themselves and acknowledging where they are spiritually, emotionally, and financially, probably because they do not want to confront their weaknesses.

God knows you better than you know yourself and loves you just the way you are. Nevertheless, self-assessment is the first step toward progress. You cannot make any progress in the race of life if you deny where you are right now. I see this often in street evangelism; people have a hard time committing their lives to Jesus Christ simply because they don't think they are sinners or refuse to admit they have done anything wrong.

When God came into the garden after Adam and Eve sinned, He asked Adam a question to help him assess his situation. Here is God's question and Adam's response: *"Then the LORD God called to Adam and said to him, 'Where are you?' So he said, 'I heard your voice in the garden, and I was afraid because I was naked; and I hid myself' "* (Gen. 3:9–10).

God is omnipresent, which means He is everywhere at the same time. He definitely knew Adam's physical location. Nevertheless, He asked him this question: "Where are you?" God didn't ask this question because He couldn't find Adam, but rather, God wanted Adam to acknowledge his spiritual position. In essence, God said, "Adam, I know where you are, but do you?"

Even today, God still asks the same question of us: "Where are you?" Until we answer this question, we will never understand the adjustments necessary to finish the race strong.

BE FOCUSED

We are living in a generation that is easily distracted and sidetracked. The enemy offers many options to divert us from running the race before us. I am convinced that distraction is one of the enemy's end-time weapons that he uses against the church and the people of God. Distraction births procrastination, and procrastination results in unfruitful lives because we push aside the things that would propel us to our destinies in order to make room for useless distractions.

The problem with many of us is simply that we have not set any priorities in life. Everything draws the same level of attention in our eyes. We might not verbally admit this, but we certainly act like it. But we need to be focused in life, and in order to be focused, we need to set priorities.

The apostle Paul said, "This one thing I do." My question to you is, how many things do you do? What is the focus of your life? You must have one thing at the top of your list of priorities and let everything else revolve around it, and that one thing must be the kingdom of God. As Jesus said in Matthew 6:33, *"Seek first the kingdom of God and His righteousness, and all these things shall be added to you."*

The kingdom of God must be the primary focus in the life of any believer. Whatever we do (career, school, ministry, studies, family) must yield a kingdom impact and effect. Jesus pointed His disciples to this one thing. In Paul's life, everything he did was for the sole purpose of advancing the kingdom of God. My question to you is, are you kingdom oriented or world oriented? Is your focus on chasing God or chasing after things?

Each and every one of us must review our priorities in life.
Matthew 6:33 provides a clear template of the things that are important and that should be the primary focus of our lives. As Christians, our core priority should be the advancement of the kingdom. As we seek His kingdom, everything else we need will be supplied. In my own life, I have observed this pattern at work. Whenever I stay focused on advancing God's kingdom, I experience favor in the other areas of my life.

Whenever we focus on one thing, we sacrifice anything that competes with that focus. This is what Nehemiah did in the rebuilding of the wall of Jerusalem: *"So I sent messengers to them, saying, 'I am doing a great work, so that I cannot come down. Why should the work cease while I leave it and go down to you?' but they sent me this message four times, and I answered them in the same manner"* (Neh. 6:3–4).
Many things compete for our attention. If we allow anything

and everything to catch our attention, we will never accomplish our God-given assignments. But if we remain focused, we will always excel.

The purpose of distraction is to make us unproductive, delay the fulfillment of God's purpose, or even to prevent the accomplishment of His plan. The Bible says they sent messengers to Nehemiah four times to try to persuade him to come down from the wall. Whenever we are doing a great work for God, we must always be careful of the things demanding our attention from the task at hand.

FORGETTING THE PAST

Isaiah 43:18–19 says, *"Do not remember the former things, nor consider the things of old. Behold, I will do a new thing, now it shall spring forth; shall you not know it? I will even make a road in the wilderness and rivers in the desert."*

Every person has a background following him or her wherever he or she goes. Your past can serve you well once you understand its importance and how to handle it as you journey toward your future. Unfortunately, many people are stuck on their journeys to their destinies because they mishandle their past experiences.

The apostle Paul gives us the proper way of dealing with the past: forget it! When Paul speaks about forgetting the past, he means we should not live in the past or dwell on it. If we want to reach the next level in our personal lives, businesses, or ministries, we need to learn to let go of the past.

Every time we live in our past, we live without God, since He is always in the present. He told Moses to tell the people of Israel that He was "I AM," not I WAS. As long as we keep looking backward, we can never see our way forward. In turn, this will prevent us from going to where God is waiting for us. Remember, God is not in the past, but in the present.

Every person on the earth has two kinds of pasts: past failures and past successes.

Past Failures

In my years of ministry, I have discovered that past failure is one of the most common strongholds people—even those in the body of Christ—deal with. One of the symptoms of someone living in past failures and mistakes is that the person tries to justify his or her present situation according to the past, trying to find excuses for not moving forward in life. But just because you failed in your business, family, relationships, or ministry does not mean you cannot start over again.

Bishop T. D. Jakes and Bishop Paul Morton have recorded one of my favorite songs on a CD entitled He-Motions. The song is called "It Doesn't Matter," and it is a powerful word of encouragement for every person dwelling on past failures. Though it may seem as though you cannot move even an inch, you can walk fully in God's plan for your life if you will let go of the past.

When God wanted to destroy Sodom and Gomorrah, a place of sin, failure, deceit, and disappointment, He spared Lot and his family as a result of Abraham's prayer and intercession. But look what happened in Genesis 19:25–26: "*He overthrew, destroyed, and ended those cities, and all the valley and all the inhabitants of the cities, and what grew on the ground. But [Lot's] wife looked back from behind him, and she became a pillar of salt*" (AMP).

The lesson of this story is that whenever we turn to look at our past, we literally stop in our tracks. We stop fulfilling our purpose, we stop running the race, we stop being the man or woman God wants us to be, we stop advancing the cause of Zion. We stop reaching out to fulfill our destinies—we just come to a complete stop. No matter how painful it is, then, we need to let go of our past failures so God can take us to a better place.

Past Success

God is always in a fast-forward mode. Many times, because we have experienced God a certain way in the past, we think God will perform in the same way today. But I don't want to experience God the same way today that I did yesterday. God takes us from one level of glory to another. I don't want God to move in my ministry today the same way He did in the past—I want a fresh experience with Him.

Sadly, however, there are people who spend eternity talking about their past successes and exploits in life, despite what Isaiah 43:18–19 instructs: *"Do not remember the former things, nor consider the things of old. Behold, I will do a new thing, now it shall spring forth; shall you not know it? I will even make a road in the wilderness and rivers in the desert."* God is telling us that if they want to walk with Him and tap into the next realm, we must long to experience Him to a greater degree than we have ever experienced Him. We need to see higher and go forward.

Don't park in your former prayer life, but desire a fresh and new experience with God. Let Him challenge you more, and go deeper with Him. As Paul urged, keep moving from glory to glory with God (2 Cor. 3:18).

In our passage from Philippians, Paul said he reached for those things set before him. God has set before us ministry, souls, young adults to win and impact, nations, scholarships, marriages, kids, and many other great things. Are we reaching for all He wants to do in our lives? Hebrews 12:2, in speaking of Jesus, says, "For the joy that was set before him, [He] endured the cross." Can we say the same?

In Joshua 1:1–2, God told Joshua that Moses, His servant, was dead. One of the reasons God said this was that Joshua was still mourning the death of Moses. God is not against mourning, but He realized Joshua and the people of Israel had begun to dwell on the past and were not moving forward to lay hold of the Promised Land.

PRESS ON

When I see the word press, I picture the application of pressure to something. In a spiritual sense, it indicates that life won't always be easy, and sometimes we may feel like quitting or giving up. There will always be spiritual opposition, physical opposition, and many challenges. Nevertheless, Hebrews 12:1–2 shows us how we can press on: *"Therefore we also, since we are surrounded by so great a cloud of witnesses, let us lay aside every weight, and the sin which so easily ensnares us, and let us run with endurance the race that is set before us, looking unto Jesus, the author and finisher of our faith, who for the joy that was set before Him endured the cross, despising the shame, and has sat down at the right hand of the throne of God."* First, we need endurance, or perseverance, to continue in the race before us. Then, as we run, we look unto Jesus, staying focused on Him as our model of how to lay hold of the promise.

Paul said in Philippians 3:16, "Nevertheless, to the degree that we have already attained, let us walk by the same rule, let us be of the same mind." "Let us walk by the same rule" means the Word of God is our regulation. Everything we do must align with this Word. "Let us be of the same mind" refers to having the mind of Christ, which always says "not My will, but Yours,

Father." Seeking God's glory in everything, let us move together as one body. Let us have the same confession as God's for our lives and ministries. Only then will this end-time generation rise to accomplish the great and mighty deeds God has reserved for it.

Contact the author

Apostle Chris Fire has been travelling the globe bringing revival through crusades, conferences, teachings and mentoring.

Stay in touch with us:

CHRIS FIRE MINISTRIES

P.O BOX 6
BOYDS, MD 20841

www.Chrisfire.org
Phone: 240-232-6126

facebook.com/revivalrcm
Instagram.com/fire3chris
Tweeter.com/fire3chris
Periscope/fire3chris

Made in the USA
Middletown, DE
09 November 2023

42108403R00056